A SLICE OF LIFE

Fifty Years in Blyth Valley
The People's Perspective

Blyth Spartans Football Club 1994/95. Winners of Unibond First Division Championship Trophy

Compiled by Andy Griffin

First Published in 1996
Reprinted twice in 1997 by
Blyth Valley Borough Council
Cultural Development Section
Council Offices
Seaton Delaval
Northumberland
NE25 0DX

Cover: River Sketch by Joan Scott

Printed by Peterson Printers,12 Laygate, South Shields,Tyne & Wear, NE33 5RP

ISBN 1 898747 03 2

*Blyth Valley Borough Council gratefully acknowledges
financial assistance from Northern Arts Board.*

FOREWORD

I am pleased to introduce you to A Slice of Life. This book is the end product of a twelve month long writing project in Blyth Valley with the writer Andy Griffin. During the project Andy visited groups and individuals around the Borough and encouraged them to share their stories, memories, views and ideas about life in the Blyth Valley area over the last fifty years and right up to the present day. Around five hundred people took part altogether and over one hundred pieces of submitted work have been included in the book.

The book really is a slice of life in Blyth Valley, covering many themes and topics from work in the ship building and mining industries that are now so sadly gone, to the variety of popular entertainment and leisure pursuits. The book is a celebration of Blyth Valley and the people who live here. What comes through really strongly is the spirit of the people, the lively humour, the strength and resourcefulness, the independence and the integrity.

The writings include people from every part of the Borough, from all walks of life and from all age groups from four to ninety-four. Many of the pieces remind us of how life has changed over the last fifty years and the way things used to be. In this sense the book documents the social history of Blyth Valley. I would like to thank all those who have contributed to A Slice of Life and hope that everyone enjoys reading it as much as I have done.

Cllr George Barron

LEADER,

BLYTH VALLEY BOROUGH COUNCIL

Councillor George Barron

INTRODUCTION

My association with Blyth Valley spans several decades. As a child in the 1950's I frequently came to Blyth to visit relatives and the town always left me with a strong impression of industrial bustle. This was quite a contrast to the seasonal sea changes at Whitley Bay where my mother ran a guest house. In 1973 I came with my family to live and work in the borough and my affection for the area has grown ever since.

Blyth Valley has known difficult times over the past fifty years and there has been a decline in the region's heavy industrial base. The 1960's saw the end of Blyth's passenger railway service, the closure of the shipyards and a rationalisation of the sixteen or so mining communities in the area. During this decade Cramlington New Town emerged, bringing with it modern industrial estates. The Blyth Valley workforce, highly skilled in traditional trades, was forced to re-train to meet the needs of the local factories; not all found work and the town and villages still have a legacy of unemployment.

Circumstances may change; the people do not. There is a warmth and generosity of spirit from this North East coastal area that outsiders frequently comment on. In 1985 Jonathan Raban, the best-selling travel writer, sailed around the entire coast of Britain and wrote of his experiences in the book 'Coasting'. Of all the places he stayed at, he found Blyth, by far, the most interesting and friendly. He felt accepted and at ease from the moment he stepped ashore. I share his view.

There is however, a self-effacing side to the people, which is a strength as well as a weakness. The residents are rarely boastful or arrogant, but I feel their natural inclination to modesty has a tendency to undervalue their real achievements. It may not be the most glamorous spot in England, yet it was this area's coal and shipping that gave the nation its wealth and power; this should not be forgotten. I believe a publication to celebrate the qualities of the community is long overdue. Very little has been written about the Borough's recent past and this book has become something of a personal crusade to rectify this.

I was delighted when Helen Payne, Cultural Development Officer of Blyth Valley Borough Council allowed me the opportunity to work for a year as a Writer in Residence. My aim was to produce a book 'for the people, by the people'. During the twelve months I spoke to as many people as possible from Seaton Sluice to Seghill and Cowpen to Cramlington; the following pages contain writing and art work from over a hundred different contributors. Older inhabitants have offered a colourful and fascinating insight into the past and children as young as four years of age have written about people and places in today's community.

Interspersed with the writing and pictures, I have included post-war 'snippets' collected from the Blyth News. I believe the collection as a whole gives a contemporary and personal overview of this unique corner of England. If it encourages a pride and appreciation of Blyth Valley, then the book has served its purpose.

It has been a privilege to meet, talk with, and reproduce the writings of the residents. Everyone I contacted had a story to tell and I was grateful for their contributions. Although the limitations of this book can only offer a 'slice of life' from the towns and villages, I hope it proves to be a satisfying portion.

Andy Griffin, Compiler

September 1996

A SLICE OF LIFE

Contents

Page

James
Taylor

EARLY DAYS...

I was born at South Farm, Cramlington.

My father died in the First World War in July 1918 almost at the end of the fighting. I would have liked to have known my dad but these things happen, what can you do? I was brough up with my mam and grandparents for my first eight years. Then my mam got a house at Ridley Street in Klondyke in 1924 and I'm still living there 72 years later. People used to think they were Cramlington Colliery houses but they weren't; only three of the 199 houses belonged to the coal company. They were typical of the miners' rows with two up and two down, a wash house and toilets out the back. The roads were not made up although we could get plenty of ash from the pit to fill in the pot holes and cover the puddles.

Klondyke was named after the place in Canada where they had the famous Gold Rush and i was 100 years old in May 1996. It was a topical event at the time and as far as I know there is no direct connection although quite a few men from this area went across hoping to make their fortunes by prospecting.

My grandmother came from Cornwall when she was 11 years of age. Her family were tin miners and when they were offered jobs at the North East pits they happily agreed. This was in 1866 at a time when miners were involved in a bitter dispute. The owners brought hundreds into Cramlington by train. They had no idea they were being used as strike-breakers, but what could they do? They were stuck here. They had to work but that didn't go down too well with the locals. When the evictions started, the idea was to put the Cornish folk into the company houses but there was such an outcry that they had to move the incomers into the school a Shankhouse instead. The Cornish folk slept there, all of them. There was no going out to socialise, they just stayed together for security. The police and the military escorted them to and from their workplace; they had to keep the factions apart otherwise there would have been bloodshed.

During all this trouble my grandma was abandoned. She was left to fend for herself - aged 11! Fortunately a sympathetic family took her in. The dispute was eventually settled but the southerners were still seen as the enemy. The local miners went back to the pit and the Cornishmen's protection was removed. They were disowned by the very people who'd brought them north and they were left to live and work in a hostile community - there was no repatriation. In time of course, the bitterness was forgotten and as the outsiders became more familiar, they were accepted and absorbed into the villages. By then there was plenty of work to go around at the seventeen or so collieries that lay within walking distance of Cramlington Village.

Eventually more houses were built and my grandma moved into 94 Shankhouse Terrace. It wa from here that she met and married my grandfather, Billy Johnson the farmer, who was the steward at South Farm. The land was owned by the coal company and it was in the farmhous that I was born.

People tell me that Billy Johnson was a hard worker and a good boss. He had loyal 'hinds' [workers] and they respected him. Twice a year he would go to the Hirings; one at Newcastle and the other at Morpeth. The farmers found their hinds from the assortment of men and women that gathered there. Workers were bought and sold, a bit like the cattle. Granda went, but he never hired anyone, he never needed to, he just went for the occasion. John Timmler and I used to take him by cart to the station early in the morning then we would come home and put a clean bale of straw in the back for when we collected him. It was usually after dark and we had to help him onto the back of the cart by lamplight and lie him on the straw. This was the only time he was ever the worse for drink; twice a year at the Hirings. He might not have been in control of his senses but he never forgot to bring me home a packet of sweets and they were always in his pocket.

He was very fair with his men. If one of the hinds said "Billy, can I have a couple of turnips?" he would deliver them himself along with a bag of potatoes. He would often give the mens' families extras. But if any of his workers took things without asking, that was it. They didn't come back the next day.

He used to work outdoors in my dad's old army putties; the ones he died in. He never bothered with Wellington boots but he always wore his son's leggings.

Arthur Heayns Klondyke

A farm productivity demonstration drew 200 farmers and agricultural experts to Laverock Hall Farm, Blyth. [*June 1953*]

Wheatridge Farm Workers 1928 Seaton Delaval

Kramel Kid [Extract]

My grandad was Cornish and my grandmother came from Devon but they married at East Cramlington Methodist Church. They came to Cramlington 52 years before I was born. My grandad had been a copper and tin miner and he had travelled the length of the country looking for work. Lots of local families are descended from that South-West corner of England. I was born in 1918 at Ridley Street, Klondyke. There were six streets then, named after the local personages: Percy, Hastings, Ridley and Storey. Water came from standpipes in each street; at times we had to queue for it.

There were three shops at Klondyke. A shoe shop, a grocers and a hardware store, all owned by the James' family. One of the family hired out horse-drawn cabs, wagonettes and landaus. I often used to call on the young James' girls and we would play 'Lords and Ladies' in these posh carriages.

On this day I knocked on their door to see if they wanted to play in the cabs, when a joiner who had been constructing a dormer window on the roof above, fell off and landed at my feet. At that moment Mrs James opened the door and she collapsed into a dead faint when she saw the man lying there. It was fortunate that the joiner didn't land on me. I believe he only suffered a broken arm.

My Aunt Bessie and Uncle Bill had a fish and chip shop at Klondyke and my father often used to serve there. I would sit on the floor out of the way. When the King George picture hall came out they would all pile in for their 'six pennorth' fish supper. I got mine free.

When the Aged Miners' Cottages were being built at Klondyke, my friends and I were very brave. We climbed over the fence and went into the houses to look around. But when Sandy the village bobby appeared on the horizon, we had to scarper and I tore my hands on the pointed tops of the military fence. At home I had some explaining to do and my dad got his black belt out. I was there when the cottages were opened by Newcastle United's star player Hughie Gallagher, and they are still standing today although the stone footballs which were on top of the gate posts have long since gone.

We had a cat called Daisy and Dad used to put her out every night. She would immediately jump up onto the roof, climb over the ridge to the front of the house and cry at our skylight window. We would open the skylight and let her into bed with us. Father found out eventually. More black belt!

We had netties of course and these 'earth closets' were just a wooden seat with an oval hole in it, with a smaller hole for the children. When I was an apprentice joiner I learned how to mark out these oval shapes by using a piece of string and two nails but I never yet found out how the size of the holes was decided upon. The 'middens men' cleaned out the netties each week with shovels, and a horse and cart would transport it to the 'Dolly Heap' at the top end of our street. In the summer we would give it a wide berth. The heap is still there today, covered with luscious grass, so it should be, it was well manured!

Between the wars all the villages of Cramlington were self-contained. Each had their own pub, shops, chapel, schools, miners' welfare - even their own football team. Hartford, Shankhouse, East Cramlington, West Cramlington, South Cramlington; they each had their own individual identity but shared one thing in common: coal! They were miles from the old peaceful village centre with its three farms: East, West and Middle. The old village had two pubs, a Methodist chapel and a C of E church. Each community was connected by footpaths through the fields.

Leslie Miners Cramlington

A new wonder organic manure (superior to the best 'farmyard') is being manufactured by Blyth Corporation at a purpose-built composting plant in Cowpen [*December 1961*]

A Rural View 1990's

Dad [Extract]

A large assortment of vegetables were grown for family and friends in our big corner garden. Like all good gardeners, Dad grew things in strict rotation and woe betide any weed that dared rear its head on his territory. All the relatives on Dad's side of the family were kept supplied and he even made occasional week-end trips to Yorkshire in which he carried vegetables and tightly-packed bundles of firewood for my maternal grandmother. Dad's bundles were about six times the size of the puny little packs sold in local shops. I used to watch him tying them up and actually hammering in a few extra sticks to compact them even more.

A short distance away from the house were the allotments. Some men grew vegetables or flowers on these garden plots but Dad kept his hens there. He had several hen-houses (crees) and from an early age I was taken with him and given little jobs to do. I liked throwing the corn down for the hens to peck at (I did not like the cockerel) but when I was older, and told to collect eggs from the crees, I was not quite so happy. Each nest-box had a soft cover hanging down in front of it with an opening for the hen to see out of, and for the collector to put their hand in to retrieve the eggs. If the box was empty of all but the straw I had no problem but if the occupier was in residence that was a very different matter. I had been instructed in the correct way to remove the egg by putting my hand very gently under the hen and easing it out. Coward that I was, it just needed the hen to look at me with those bright beady eyes, or open its spike-like beak, and I would quickly move to the next box, empty-handed. I loved the soft brown feathers and their croaky clucks but drew the line at anything else. When I returned to Dad from my collecting, he knew how many eggs there should have been, there was no fooling him. He used to joke and tell me I was a softie. He was not wrong.

The thing I enjoyed most in connection with Dad's hens was when he put eggs into the incubator and tended them until they hatched. The incubator stayed in Mam and Dad's bedroom; it was a piece of furniture made of a rich russet-coloured wood. It had four long slender legs topped with a shallow box-like glass section. Mam took as much pride in keeping the legs of the incubator as highly polished as she did her other furniture.

Sometimes I used to follow Dad upstairs when he put the eggs in and he explained to me that there would soon be chicks hatching out. An inseparable part of Dad was a short, stubby indelible pencil and a dog-eared little notebook, both of which were kept in his railway waistcoat pocket. When there were eggs in the incubator he would write things in his book then turn the eggs and mark a cross on some of them. When the eggs began to hatch I would be lifted up to see what was happening. The shell would crack from inside and after what seemed a very long time to me, a chick would emerge. After its very exhausting struggle, there it would lie, wet and bedraggled. (Today, whenever I see a Yorkshire Terrier, I am always reminded of the first glimpse of a new chick.) Dad would gently lift them out of the incubator and take them downstairs to the kitchen. There they were popped into a box lined with a soft piece of old blanket that was placed by the fireside. As they recovered from their ordeal they soon became the soft, fluffy, yellow chicks we all recognise. The noise of the cheeping from such small creatures reached an unbelievable crescendo.

When the hatching was over, the chicks were transferred by Dad into the brooder, which was in a cree in the back garden. This kept them warm and safe until they were strong enough to be transferred to the pullet's cree at the allotment. I was told many years later that on more than one occasion a chick had to be rescued from my 'kind' attention. I did love them so - and I was very small.

As I grew older, I suppose I must have been about six years old, my Saturday job was to take eggs to friends and relatives. I did my deliveries on a small two-wheeler bike (in those days they were called fairy cycles). One day a big dirty Airedale dog knocked me off and my last half-dozen eggs were broken. I went on my weeping journey to my Aunt Lucy's who took pity on me, paid me the money and said it would be our little secret. I have always had a special feeling for this lady.

Dorothy Redpath   Blyth

~ Potato Plant ~

Tetty Picking

By late September the fruit on hedgerow bramble bushes was ripe and heavy and this meant one thing; the Blackberry Week school holidays. To the boys it meant 'tetty pickin' week. Hartley Main Collieries owned some local farms as well as the pits and Lysdon, Lookout, Wheatridge and Avenue farms were all hiring tetty pickers.

On his first morning, Ben came downstairs to bacon, egg and fried bread. His eyes widened at the feast; it was usually porridge or bread and jam. His mam was smiling.

"Working men have to have a good meal under their belts."

Ben kept his pail tucked under the table as he ate. He had a 7:30 start at the Lookout farm and he wasn't going to be late.

The boys were jostling and laughing as they heard their names read out and they filed onto the two long corn carts ready to be taken to the potato fields. On arrival they were sorted into couples. A farm labourer carefully paced out equal portions of furrowed land and stuck in twigs at various points. This accurate measuring was of great importance to the boys because the distance between the twigs was their working patch. Any discrepancy between the sticks could mean more work for some and less for others. Ben and his pal Tommy had heard of many bitter quarrels caused by the stealthy moving of these markers.

Soon, large hessian bags were thrown from the carts and orders were given:

"Big potatoes in one bag, small and medium into the other."

Ben looked down the length of the field that disappeared into the distance. It was 8:15, the sky was blue and the sun warm. It was great to be alive.

The horse started forward, pulling a whirring digger which revolved the spoon-like shovels that caught under the rotten shaws and threw the white potatoes to the surface. From now on it was heads down and bums up. The farm labourer and his mate watched the youngsters on their first day. It was hard work with the digger going down one furrow, then a gap, then up the other. The only rest the boys could snatch was when the digger went between the furrows. For this back-breaking work Ben received one shilling and sixpence [7.5p] per day, plus a pailful of potatoes.

All week the lads worked and by late Saturday morning they had finished the farm's potato crop. It was a proud day for Ben as he handed his Mam 9/6d [47.5p]. His week's wages.

Tom Humphrey Seaton Sluice

Zeppelin

I was two years old when there was a visit from a German Zeppelin that created panic in the area. For several hours it flew above the villages and dropped bombs between Blyth and Wallsend. We were still at war with Germany in 1918.

There were postcards issued at the time of this visit which shows the people in Blyth market place going about their daily lives, seemingly oblivious of the massive deadly airship over their heads. The truth is, the population were terrified. I could never understand how people could look so calm until someone told me that the cards were the result of trick photography. The manufacturers superimposed pictures of the Zeppelin onto existing views to cash in on such a major event.

Resident Blyth

Zeppelin Postcard

ombshell

> Blyth labourer John Harthill was saved from falling 40 feet onto jagged rocks at Seaton Sluice by holding onto an unexploded bomb protruding from the cliff-face. [*Nov. 1959*]

During the Second World War a German bomber lost its way at night and flew down the River Blyth to try and find the submarine base and the shipyard. For some reason the air-raid sirens didn't go and without warning the pilot dropped his bombs over Blyth station. They scored a direct hit on a signal box and destroyed a set of railway carriages. Mayhem followed.

I was at home in the kitchen at the time with my mam. She was sitting on a cracket when suddenly this piece of wheel flange came through the roof - from over a quarter-of-a-mile away! It hit my mother a glancing blow on the shoulder and completely smashed the wooden stool she had been sitting on. The air-raid wardens came to help and they insisted that my mam should go to the Miners' Welfare Hall on Renwick Road (now the Civic Centre) for medical attention. She refused because it meant leaving her family, and in those days there was no way that she would leave us on our own. She had regrets about it later because after that incident she had a bad back for the rest of her days. Had she reported her injury then she would have qualified for a war pension.

Tommy Robertson Blyth

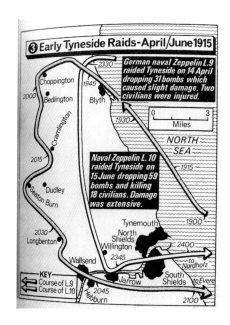

A farewell dance was given by HM Submarine Seraph which had been at Blyth during the war years. [*October 1946*]

£10,000 is raised by residents towards a war memorial at Seaton Sluice. [*Dec. 1949*]

Blyth Beach

Old Chain Ferry

WHATEVER HAPPENED TO GOOD OLD BLYTH

Do you remember good old Blyth?
Hoot Gibson walking the beat?
When lads and lasses played muddy kiddy
And relievo in the street.
The neighbours used to really care
And ask if you were copin'
And when you did your shopping
You left the back door open.
On Sunday night folk went in droves
To walk along the prom
Or others would go to Ridley park
Where the brass band music came from.

Blyth had a passenger train
On a popular railway line
And the bus fare up to Newcastle
Was less than 'one and nine'.
You crossed the river by ferries
For decades they stood the test:
The squat wire-roped 'High' ferry
The 'Low' and the one that went west.
The event of the year was the carnival
With floats and bands on parade
Proceeds went to the hospital
For the Knight Memorial aid.

Hedley and Youngs was a classy shop
And Skees sold goods to the sailors
And men could get a real good suit
From the Fifty Shillings Tailors.
There was 'Willsey' Heron, optician
Selling specs at a moderate price,
On the other side of Waterloo Road
Was the chemists and Harry Fordyce.
And thru'pence could buy you fish and chips
Served in a pleasant manner
And everything at Woolworths
Would cost you less than a 'tanner'.

Most of our cinemas had to close down
When interest in Bingo grew
The Essoldo, Roxy, Theatre Royal
And Central Cinema too.
The Alexandria Billiards Hall
With the 'Mounts' looking after the games;
Billiards and snooker and Russian pool
And others with more fancy names.
Remember the Tudor Ballroom?
You could get a really good dance,
Young people used to behave themselves
And many found time for romance.

The shipyard was fully-employed then,
Working on ships old and new
And hundreds of bikes flew down Regent Street
When the shipyard buzzer blew.
The miners worked hard for their money
And got 'six and ninepence' a shift.
Big families to feed, the miners' wives
Knew the meaning of thrift.
And the men coming home in their work gear
Black-faced through the colliery gate
With the little bairns all shouting out
"Have you got any left-over bait?"

They all worked hard in the family
But still found time for chit chat
As neighbours would come in and help
To finish the new proggy mat.
The women would make their own bread
With a Master Baker's skill.
Remember the smell of the stotties
As they cooled freshly-baked on the sill?
There'd be smiles down at the allotments
When the men planted turnips and 'tetties'
But by gum it was cold on a winter's night
When you crossed the road to the netties!

Who will forget Ballast Hill;
Boyd's Dairy and Boast's chandler shop?
And the dreary prison-like lodging house
Where the homeless and tramps used to flop.
The bakers often had 'biscuit boys'
Roaming around the streets
And their cries could be heard quite clearly
Selling buns or lovely 'SCEETS!'
The Sunday tea was quite a treat
With scones and lemon curd
The children, strictly disciplined,
Were 'seen but never heard'.

There's Woolcos now, and Prestos
And other cut-price stores
They've squeezed out all the little shops
That thrived between the wars.
But when we sigh for good-old-days
When everything seemed fine
We still can keep our standards
The choice is yours and mine.
Whatever happened to good old Blyth?
Change takes place of course;
But if we are to change, make sure
The change is for better .. not worse!

Charles M Mills Ellington

With the end of clothing coupons there is no rush to buy suits or costumes [Feb. 1949]
There are queues to buy sweets now they are no longer rationed. [April 1949]

Blyth Power Station

ON THE STREET...

MY GORD

When aa wuz a bairn aboot sivin year aad,
Sumbody giv iz a gord
An when aa tuk it oot in the back lane ti play
Aa tell ye, aa felt like a lord.

Me fatha he worked fo' the L.N.E.R.
Got a workmate ti mek iz a hook
An when aa went oot wi me hook an me gord
Aal the bairns cum aroond for a look.

Aa wuz up in the mornins afore it wuz lite
Boolin me gord up an doon
Me an the gord went aal ower the place
Aa wuz the happiest bairn in the toon.

Then one day sum youngins got ower the waal
Tuk me gord from its nail in the yard
An me mutha sez "Pet, divvint bubble see much."
An me Dad sez "Fo' bairns, life is hard..."

"... but if aa got me hands on the kids what did this,
By Gox, aad gi them such a clout!"
An when Plodger saw me wi me eyes red wi bubblin,
He giz three cigarette cards... for nowt.

But after a few games o' muggies an hiddney
The loss of me gord seemed ti fade,
Moont the cuddy an tiggy an pitchy-on helped
An them other back-lane games wi played.

Aa wuz sat on the kerb wedgin clay fo' a midgie
Coz aa wanted ti play 'Shine the Low'
When aa sees this fella gan past on ees bike,
A blacksmith bi the name o' Joe Howe.

He gans into wor street an up ti wor hoose
An aa sees him gan in thru wor door
Wi this greet nashin parcel tucked under ees arm
An aa sez ti meesell "Whees that for?"

Then me Mam shoots "Cum in noo, its time for ya tee,
What a state ya in, where hev ye been?"
When aa gets in thi yard, on a nail, on the waal,
Waz the biggist gord aa'd ivvor seen.

So aa sez "Dad, did Mr Howe fetch it?"
He sez "Aye an aa paid one and three."
Then Plodger pipes up "If ya playin wi ya gord
You can gi' ya clay midgie ti me."

So aa'm up in the mornins as soon as it's lite
Thez not many youngins as glad,
Aa'm back on the streets wi me hook an me gord
Thanks ti five thrupenny bits.. an me Dad

John Stenhouse Blyth

The Bella

I often played on the Bella heap with my pals. We would sit on sheets of lino floor-covering (we called it 'tarry toot') and we'd pull it over our feet and 'sledge' down the dry slag slope. I remember losing control once and ending up in the filthy stream that was known as the 'yellow babby'. I was covered and the smell was terrible. I got wrong that day!

East Hartford

In Chestnut Avenue there was still gas lamps in the early 1950's and the man that lit them would begin in our street then go from lamp to lamp in a circuit that came back to where he started from. We thought it was great shunning the lampposts and putting out the light. I was caught doing that once; I got a hiding for that as well.

Talking of lampposts, there was a miner who lived down our street and every Friday night without fail he would come home drunk. We used to see him stagger up the street using the lampposts for support. He would aim for these fixed points and lurch and stumble from one post to the next until he reached home. We watched from the window and after he passed by, we would go out and pick up all the loose change that had dropped out of his pocket. On Saturday morning we would go round to his house and give it back to him and he would always give us a thru'penny bit. This happened often. Our neighbour was never violent and everyone knew him as a God-fearing, hard-working family man - apart from Friday night! I suppose he needed to release something.

Mick Davison Blyth

Dumping Coals

At the Hartley Mains depot at Seaton Delaval there was a hopper which was full of coal. The coal lorry would load up here then deliver a supply of free coal to every colliery worker in the neighbourhood. The lorry dumped its load outside the houses and the coals had to be shovelled through the holes halfway up the walls and into the coal house. This was a bit of a chore for the men and their wives but for a tanner (2.5p) there might be lads around who would do the job. A simple little feller used to follow the truck around and offer his services with a shovel. One day he was in Double Row when the coals were dumped but the family were out. Nevertheless he set about the back-breaking job of shovelling in the coals and he called back a day or two later for his money. The woman of the house said that she hadn't asked him to shift the coal, so no, he couldn't have his tanner. Without another word, he went into the coal house and shovelled them all out again.

Tom 'Tot' Allan Seaton Delaval

Delivery

The coal was delivered outside the front door in Hunter Avenue. There would be piles after a delivery all along the length of the street. People used wheelbarrows or buckets to take it around the back. I can remember a late afternoon when it was beginning to freeze and the winter sun was a fiery orange. The loads took on a murky appearance as the light faded and the shadows of the houses slanted across the road. All that could be heard was the scraping of shovels as my neighbours tried to get the stuff in by dark.

Brian Watson Cramlington

Front Street, Bebside 1900's

Front Street, Bebside, continues to be a stopping off place for motorists to admire one of the 'prettiest thoroughfares in Northumberland'. With aspidistras in the neatly-curtained windows, it is a tribute to the elbow grease of miners' wives. [*January 1949*]

Play In The Street

As a young child I remember playing out in the street. There was a whole group of us who had known each other from an early age. Summer holidays were the best; playing out from first thing in the morning until last thing at night. There is one particular time that stands out in my mind.

All of us in the street decided to put on a pantomime for the adults. We chose 'Cinderella'. Days were spent writing out the scripts and for hours we argued about who was going to play who. It seemed everyone wanted to be Cinderella.

Weeks were spent in rehearsing and preparing costumes, especially the ballgowns whic ended up being old party dresses or our mam's long nighties with flowers tied onto the sleeve:

Invitations were sent out to parents and other adults in the street and on the Sunday befor we went back to school, the show was performed.

When the big day arrived, everyone was excited. Seats were set out in the back garden an costumes laid in the front room. Once the chairs were filled the show began.

It wasn't perfect, and not surprisingly, there were a few times when one of us forgot our line or came in at the wrong time, but amazingly we made it to the end. It all went down extremel well with the few spectators, so too did the cups of orange juice after the performance.

We were all pleased when it was over and relieved it was a success and just like in th fairytales, 'we all lived happily ever after.'

Joanne Towers

Sixth Form, Blyth Ridley High School

Blyth man Angus Galloway caused international amusement when he spent his two-week annual holiday at the Steamboat Inn, 150 yards from his home. [*July 1968*]

Territory (1950)

In Hunter Avenue, the pit heap with the colliery railway lines, acted as a territorial divisio between the lads who lived on the south side (the Wensleydalers) and us (the Croftoners). W gathered in varying numbers on the yet unbuilt fields during the summer nights and chase each other backwards and forwards in a kind of running war. Lads from other parts of Bly would join one of the sides and try to outface the enemy. On the instruction 'Charge!' we wou either run for our lives back onto our side of the line or we would overwhelm the oppositic with our intimidating cries. It was a great victory if we could run into the streets of Wensleyda Terrace looking for rivals, but they would have all disappeared. There was never any re fighting; at most an arm might get punched in the school playground the following day.

Brian Watson Cramlington

The Duke of Northumberland officially opened the first industrial estate and residential area in Cramlington New Town; the future home for more that 40,000 residents. [*October 1964*]

DEATH

[Behind York Close in Cramlington, bedroom windows overlooked a square; a meeting place for the older rowdy kids in the area.]

It used to live
Part of the ever-changing
countdown of places to be

They sat there
On cold-bricked wall of remaining
pieces

Sometimes laughed there
All involved with the belly-aching
words of a clown

You could hear them
From a towering safe haven on a
summer's night

You could see them
From the double-paned glass, that
rebellious group

They fell there
Onto soft grassy mounds that lay beneath

I was part there
Hearing joyous roars and conversation whilst lying.

They left there
Never returning to the concrete-walled flat that is the square

And I remember
The death of an era becomes the happy memory

Michael Finch Age 13
Brockwell Middle School Cramlington

More than 900 residents of Seghill signed a petition calling for the return of the village bobby. [*April 1983*]

Dad [Extract]

As I grew older I played with my friends in the big field at the back of the house. They were a nice crowd, we had all been born in the avenue and had grown up together. There was never any problem when I played rounders or other games with the girls but as soon as a boy came onto the scene my dad would be there. He would shout me into the house. It was so unfair. I was a shy child but I did feel comfortable with these children. Was he possessive? Or just plain over-protective? I really don't know.

Dad did not go to church, but Mam did. My brother and I were sent to Sunday School. As I got older I joined the usual activities, Brownies, Girl Guides and the youth club. I actually progressed to become a Sunday School teacher, a Guider and a Tawny Owl. Dad was very proud of all these achievements. No objections were raised when I went to Camp, he liked my friends; girls, I hasten to add.

Dorothy Redpath Blyth

HOME FROM WORK

Airbrushed sky,
clear,
shining sleek as chrome;

Trees motionless,
branches hanging dull
as dreadlocks;

Streetlights hesitating
from pink to amber,
House lights
raw as a wound;

A rash of starlings
chase each other to roost;

Holywell Village

I carry with me the cold
aroma of winter
into my child's embrace.

Roger McDonald
Holywell

Fir Cones

My house has a dozen fir trees on the front green.

It looks lovely when the snow lies on their branches.

When it is near Christmas we go and collect the fir cones and put glitter on them then hang them on our Christmas tree inside the house. We tie them carefully to the branches so we don't knock off the other decorations.

With the presents under the tree and red tinsel all around our white marble fireplace, it looks really Christmassy.

In summer the resin on the trees gets really sticky. Sometimes we go under them for the shade but they are prickly now. When I was little I used to climb them. I thought they were huge. One of them is now as big as our house. From the window it looks like Christmas all the year round.

Jeunine Thompson Age 11

St Peter's Middle School, Cramlington.

> Traffic at Hodgson's Road was diverted for two hours when a 130 feet long, 22 ton steel girder which was being moved from Blyth Shipyard to the Kitty Brewster bridge site slipped on its trailer. *[August 1960]*

FROM AN OPEN BEDROOM WINDOW
[Hunter Avenue, Blyth 1945]

Silence?
Almost.

A dog barks distantly.
Intermittent wind
rattles the window
on its latch.

Tall poplars from the Jordan's garden
sway
a myriad rustling of branches and leaves
ceaselessly stirring
never still.

Last coastal buses.
Tyres singing their high notes
on dry runs.
Swishier
when wet.

Occasional farm sounds:
Chickens and turkeys
brought in snatchy gusts
by the
Westerly.

Clear or dim
Blyth's lighthouse foghorn
with its three-in-a-row blarings,
forty seconds apart.
Distant Souter Point;
mistily,
foggily,
emits a single drone.

A vague jangle from Crofton Mill Pit.
The Tankie
shunts
and links
the line of trucks;
a cascading
metal buffeting.

This side of the pit heap;
early wet washing
flaps and cracks
in windswept gardens.

Brian Watson Cramlington

The Coronation celebrations in the Borough defied continuous rain. [*June 1953*]
Blyth Valley is decked out in red, white and blue to celebrate the marriage of Prince Charles to Lady Diana. [*July 1981*]

Staithes

In the 1950's we lived in a Georgian house at Wensleydale Terrace in Blyth and my younger brother and sister were born there. Beyond the back garden was Wright's timber yard and at the side of the house was the railway line that led to the staithes. A bridge took the trucks over the road at rooftop level and the embankment ended at our garden. It also happened to be on the bend that went behind Ridley Park so it was noisy right through the day but we were so used to it we never noticed. Between the house and the line was our garden. Looking at it today, it is just a small patch of lawn but we used to call it the field and all the kids in the neighbourhood would come and play here. There was never any danger from the line although in a dry summer we occasionally had to put out fires in the garden as sparks from the cornering engines would set the grass alight.

David Phillipson Tynemouth

Staithes

A sustained blizzard cuts the Borough off from Tyneside with no newspapers or mail getting through; even food supplies are threatened. When miners of Hartford returned home as no work was available due to the winter conditions, they cleared the village of snow [*March 1947*]

The Avenues

We moved to Hunter Avenue in Blyth when I was very small. The house had lain empty for several months, the walls were painted bright red and the bath had been used to keep coal in. One of the major attractions was that it had electricity. My father was working as a painter for the council on the massive Housing Scheme which was the construction of The Avenues. I believe they took their numbers from the sequence in which they were built, starting with First Avenue, Second Avenue and so on to Twenty-sixth. I can understand why there is no 13th Avenue but what happened to 16th, 17th, 19th, 21st and 24th? I suppose someone has an explanation.

Brian Watson Cramlington

Mr J W Stafford of Eighth Avenue, Blyth, retired as a postman after fifty years in which he has walked 75,000 miles [*April 1947*]

12th Avenue

Why is it, that if I meet anyone new, as soon as I mention that I live in 12th Avenue they take a step back, as if they don't want to know any more?
What is so wrong with 'The Avenues'?
OK, maybe there are newer places to live but I have no desire to move there. My house is my home and I like my street just the way it is.
I could not ask for a nicer place, with friendly people who get along just fine. Where I live there is no ill-feeling between any of our neighbours so why do people take a second glance as soon as I say the word 'Avenue'?
In my avenue, everyone knows everyone, and we always do each other favours whenever they are needed. If anyone goes on holiday we will look after their house and pop in to open and close the curtains.
The street often has a party atmosphere. If any neighbours have good news, they share it and we all go round to make the most of the night.

A couple of us have dogs and if we meet on the field we will stop for a chat because we get along well with each other - even if the dogs don't!

People moan and groan and shout about their neighbours saying:
'They play their music too loud.' or 'They're driving me mad.' But not me! My neighbours are great. I have a lovely old lady living next door to me and she treats me like her own granddaughter.

So you see, next time you meet someone from The Avenues, don't stereotype us. We are a friendly collection of individuals living happily together. It's my home and I wouldn't change it.

Nicki Ormston
Sixth Form, Blyth Ridley High School

Floods

Housewives in Cowpen Quay were 'living in dread' and demanding protection as the town experiences its worst flooding for many years. [*November 1954*]

We lived in Regent Street and every autumn and spring we would get the high tides. Twice a year our house was under water. It didn't flood in from the river banks, it simply seeped through the floor - you could do nothing about it. Into the 1960's the dreaded flooding was a constant misery. I remember one morning coming downstairs bleary-eyed to suddenly find myself knee deep in water! The tide had come up through the night. We had to move the furniture upstairs and bail out. When the water subsided we put fires on in every room to dry out the walls and floor; for days the smell of damp was terrible. We always had a tide mark above the skirting board two feet [60 cm] from the floor. Naturally we complained about the problem and at long last we had a visit from our local politician. By this time we had dried the rooms out but the

Park Road Floods, Blyth

permanent tide line was visible. He came into our living room, tapped the walls, told us there was nothing wrong with the houses, then turned round and walked out again. Good solid buildings he said, and that was that! We were speechless.

Once our neighbours went on holiday and left me the key. Sure enough the tides were high so I had to remove all their furniture and carpeting to the upstairs landing to stop them getting ruined. That took some doing! A week or so later the neighbour came knocking on the door shouting 'Eddie, we've been burgled.' They'd just come back home and saw their living room was empty. I'd forgotten all about it.

When it was at its worst, the water would flood across the road and every time the traffic went past it would send waves into our living room. It got so bad that my uncle [Charles Long] and a few neighbours, blocked the road and asked the motorists, particularly the bus drivers, if they would make a detour up Goschen Street. They were all reasonable, nobody objected - apart from the police. I guess they were bound by regulations but they were unwilling to bend the rules. They arrived and told my uncle that he had no authority to divert vehicles and they insisted that they continue past our house. There was hell on that day. Fortunately the neighbours came out in force and stood behind my uncle but it was touch and go - they nearly arrested him and bundled him off to the police station. He would stand up to anybody if he thought he was right. That's why he had such respect from the shipyard workers; as a shop steward, he fought every step of the way for them.

We were still living in the houses when the local estate agents sold them off to a private concern. When the new owners came round to inspect their purchases Uncle Charlie tried to warn them and he took them to one side and asked:

'What are you going to do about the floods?'

'Don't worry' they said reassuringly, 'we're going to fit a damp course.'

Shortly afterwards the houses were demolished and in the 1970's the streets of Blyth were dug up to make way for a massive £4m flood drainage scheme.

Eddie Cain Blyth

An incredible downpour transformed Blyth into another Venice in just 15 minutes. Mrs Margaret Phillipson almost drowned in her car as it became engulfed in water on Newsham Road.
[*August 1980*]

Tom, aa knaa where thaa's weels fo' a bogie.
Thaa's an owld pram just been hoyed away,
It's on the heep, an the tires luk gud,
So aa think we shud gan strite away.
Aa kin get a bit plank off me Gran-da,
An a big wuddin box from the Store,
A bit of owld rope off the claes line
An that cushin we used once before.

Me Daa's got sum nails in the coal-hoose
An aa think thaa's a big nut an bowlt.
Wi kin born the front hole wi the poker
An fit shaft fo' ti get a gud howld.

Can ye cadge sum green paint from yor Malcolm?
O' tha might be a tin in the shed.
Wi kin paint the plank green an' the fut rests
An' that box'll luk champion in red.

An' once we've got it aal finished,
We'll gan ti the heep fo' ti try 'er,
We'll mek aal the youngins deed jellus,
An we'll caal it the Richard Street Flyer.

So let's dee away fo' the pram weels
Afore sum one else gets a keek,
We'll mek us the best ivver bogie,
It's the best day aa've had aal this week!

John Stenhouse
Blyth

'Nowhere have I met such friendly people as the residents in Blyth' said a German youth; one of a party of nineteen young people from Solingen who are visiting the town. [*August 1962*]

LESSONS FOR LEARNING...

MY NURSERY

I can remember
When I was small
I went to a nursery
In Hareside's hall

My Mum dropped me off
With a kiss and a smile
When my childminder came
We would talk for a while.

I had so much fun
All day I played
And when lunchtime came
I happily stayed.

I made lots of friends
With the girls and the boys
We dressed up and sang
And played with big toys.

I first learned to read
With 'Ben' and his pet
I played in the water
And got rather wet.

I loved every minute
I never wished to leave
Especially when Santa came
As it neared Christmas Eve.

I can remember
When I was small
I went to a nursery
In Hareside's hall.

Jennifer Brady Age 12
St Peter's Middle School Cramlington

Blyth Valley Education Committee was told that more schoolchildren preferred dinner at home rather than at the school canteen; this was against the national trend. [*Feb. 1952*]

I went to Princess Louise Road Secondary School until 1952. The headteacher was E W Short who became Deputy Leader of the Labour Party in Harold Wilson's cabinet. He used to walk around school in a black gown and he was often away at political meetings. I had one of my few conversations with him when I was milk monitor. It was good working on the milk because you got out of lessons to deliver the bottles to all the classes. On this particular morning a woman came in to see the headmaster so I got onto the telephone - the science teacher had rigged up this telephone system from the cloakroom to the office - so I rang him up and told him there was a wife downstairs wanting to see him. He went mad. He said 'It is a 'lady' who has come to see me, how dare you call her a 'wife'. I got a right roasting for that.

The school was strict then. Twice I got the cane for talking when we were lining up ready to go into school. The cane left your hands red and raw.

Soon after I left it became a Secondary Modern. I suppose that meant they demolished the air raid shelters in the playground and had inside toilets. I left school on the Friday, aged 15, and I started work at Crofton Mill Pit on the Monday. Most school leavers walked straight into a job.

Tommy Robertson Blyth

> Out of 464 pupils who have left school in the area only 24 failed to find employment near home or within travelling distance [*October 1958*]

PLR Boys 1950,s

Crofton Juniors [Late 1940's]

I went to Crofton Juniors in Blyth (the Big School) where Mr Redford, brother of the local butcher, was headmaster. His hair was always combed and brushed into a side parting. He wore pin-striped suits and highly polished black shoes. Miss Hope, Miss Bates and Miss Hornsby taught me at that time. We had a perky no-nonsense lady teacher when I was about eleven and I remember an incident with my classmate Joe. At the beginning of each year our names had to be called out for the register and the class laughed out loud when Joe announced his full name "Joseph Whitehouse Perry Morton." The teacher was not amused. Joe was not a trouble-maker but she threatened to tie his hands behind his back, to more hilarity. There was incredulity as the teacher opened her desk lid and pulled out a length of twine and proceeded to bind Joe's hands to his chair. She returned to the front of the class with a triumphant smirk and continued the lesson. Joseph Whitehouse Perry Morton sat in abject misery. His face was red with tears and he had a runny nose. His head of wild uncombed hair lay on his desk top as he sobbed uncontrollably. From where I sat, I could see the frayed sleeves of Joe's jacket and the bundle of hemp that loosely tied his hands. He could easily have shaken off his 'shackles' but he was a timid lad and he remained in this heaving position until the teacher chose to release him. If the purpose of the exercise was to shock the class into obedience, then the tactic worked. But we all felt for Joe that day.

At PLR [Princess Louise Road] there were a few teachers who came back from the forces and it was easy for us to get them going with tales of army life in deserts and jungles. All the male members of staff yielded the cane and the lady teachers would send boys along (it was always boys) to be punished. The science teacher hit the hardest; usually on both hands. The stinging pain made the hands numb for a good while afterwards. There were all sorts of theories on how to minimise the effects of the cane such as licking the palms and putting a hair across your hands. If you angled your hand, just before impact, that was supposed to deflect the scything blow. The science teacher, as you would expect, had a tried and tested method. He would grasp a boy's wrist and after a few practice swishes, he would swing the bamboo very firmly onto the outstretched hand. If the contact was not 'clean' he would continue until he heard the desired thwack! The canings were always public. Some lads took it without a murmur. Others howled and thrust their burning palms into their midruffs. My friend Arty used to make faces in a show of bravado as he went back to his seat. None of us dared catch his eye for fear of giggling, which would have led to a certain caning for us.

Mr Short came. He was a tall man who wore a flowing black academic gown which took the breath out of everyone's sails. We had never seen anyone like him. His voice was of an educated mellifluous tone. His style and personality were not based on the 'rule of the rod'. Everyone seemed to be respectful of him; he was so different to people you met in Blyth. If you were sent to see him, the matter would be debated and if necessary parents were brought in for further discussion. From PLR he was elected as a Labour MP for Newcastle West and later after a highly successful political career, became Lord Glenamara.

Brian Watson Cramlington

Northumberland Education Committee expressed its confidence in coping with the post-war 'bulge' which will hit Secondary Modern and Grammar schools in 1958. [*Feb. 1957*]

Teaching In Blyth

I started teaching at New Delaval Senior School [now Blyth Golf Course] in 1939 just before the war began and was appointed as a PE teacher. In a recent News Post Leader someone submitted a picture of the schools' regional netball champions for 1940. I know the year because it was chalked on the ball! It was an odd sensation seeing myself with the team (I was the smallest) in a picture taken 55 years ago. Yet I remember it vividly, mainly because it was very rare for any team in the area to successfully challenge the netball supremacy of Princess Louise Road School.

Eastlea First 1989

During the War when King George VI and the Queen came see the Ark Royal, the pupils of New Delaval School were instructed by the County Council to welcome the royal visitors. It took an hour to walk to Wensleydale Terrace with a class of children, and a lot longer coming back. Quite a distance to go for a fleeting glimpse of royalty as their car drove past along the coastal road. One thing that struck me was that the King was wearing make-up, I expect this was to conceal the fact that he was a very sick man.

Before 1939, a female teacher had to resign her post when she married, but with the outbreak of war the law changed. When male teachers joined the armed services women were expected to continue teaching. I stayed on at New Delaval when I married in 1943 but retired to have my first child a year later. When the war ended, qualified married women teachers were urgently needed and I returned to school after the birth of my children. There were advertisements in the newspapers saying 'Please come back to us' in the hope that women teachers would be tempted back into the profession.

I worked at Bedlington Station for a while in an old wooden building that was burned to the ground some years later. I cycled the three mile journey each day from Blyth and rode there in all weathers. In the rain I wore a black waterproof cape which encased me and the bike. I was wearing this and the matching sou'wester when I distinctly heard one of the pupils say "The Lone Ranger rides again." On another occasion I was struggling against a headwind as I passed Bebside School, when the impressive Mrs Maddison, a well-known Blyth personality, stepped into the road and shouted encouragingly: "You have the heart of a lion!"

I later taught at Crofton Junior School and that was a very happy period. I frequently had a class of 40 but the children were sitting at two-seater desks and facing the blackboard. I did all my teaching from a raised plinth and my high teacher's desk overlooked the class. The children were streamed by ability and I had some very enthusiastic classes. I remember a very successful topic that we did, called 'Today's Blyth by Tomorrow's Citizens.' The children were taken to major industries in the town including a visit to Bates Pit. On that occasion we were waiting in the communications room to go down into the mine and we could hear messages from the coal-face. The children stifled their giggles because the language was so ripe! When the operator warned the men about the pupils on the surface they were extremely apologetic. In fact the miners could not have been more courteous; they were anxious that we should not get our clothes dusty. Conducted tours usually lasted 20 minutes but we were underground for two hours because, as our guide told us, the children were so interested and well behaved.

The atmosphere of heavy industry reminded me vividly of my visits to the Blyth Shipyard before the war. My father, who was a foreman joiner, took me when I was a ten year old to see his place of work, and, on some thrilling occasions, to see a ship launched.

When we visited Hughes Bolckow, the shipbreaker's yard, the management actually laid on a party for the children. On another occasion we were treated to a trip on the busy River Blyth in the pilot's boat and that was a memorable experience. I was very impressed with the way that local industry gave their time to the children and were truly glad to see them.

Another project was to improve the environment following the pit closures. Mr Manchee from County Hall was responsible for this task and no-one could have done more to improve the spoil waste areas. My class, with Mr Manchee's guidance, were responsible for a scheme in which 500 trees were planted on Crofton Mill Pit Heap. The project was years ahead of its time. It was an exciting period restoring the landscape. We also 'surveyed' the Isabella Heap and were shown pieces of 'fool's gold'. At the time, I suggested that the slag-heap should be re-named Isabella Rise but that was soon dismissed. "It will always be Bella Heap!" said one of the locals.

Jean Reid Blyth

The Duke Of Kent visits Blyth Wellesley Nautical School (Pre-1939)

Schoolteachers in Blyth sign a petition of protest against a by-law that will ban children from delivering newspapers [November 1949]

St Paul's First School

I remember the walk to my school.
Round the corner
The sun beating down on my head
And my lunch box
Half-trailing along the ground.

I remember the wooden school gates
And children swinging on them.
The yard with the old worn painted patterns
For us to play on.

I remember the classroom
With the long dragging walk
Up marble stairs.
Friends and enemies running past me
Pushing and shoving
Trying to be first.

I remember the teacher
And the grey hair
Towering over us at the front of the class
Handing out work
To anyone talking.

I remember the bell,
Sounding shrill
As we poured out of the classroom
Grabbing our coats on the way
Speeding down the stairs
Out of the door
And home
As quick as possible..

To prepare for the next day.

Andrew Ramsay Age 12
St Peter's Middle School, Cramlington

Headmaster of Blyth Grammar School, Mr J L Lloyd, sent teacher Maureen Dickerson (23) home because he considered her mini skirts were too short. She returned after ten days. [*December 1969*]

Headmaster of Blyth Grammar School, Mr J L Lloyd, received an OBE in the New Year honours list [*January 1970*]

School Visit

It was early morning when I came to school.

Mrs Bangs did the register and we talked to Mr Griffin.

After that we went back to our seats and put our coats on and Mrs Bangs called out which children were with a certain adult. My partner was Jenny.

As we went out Mrs Bangs gave us a sketch pad, a pencil, a clip board and a map. Me and Jenny clipped the map into the clip board then slipped our sketch books into the pocket of the clip board then we were ready to leave.

On the way we filled in the map and helped each other with the answers.

When we reached the River Blyth I looked carefully at the scene all around me. I decided to draw the Alcan hoppers and halfway through I thought, this is really hard.

Rachael Fletcher Age 8

Blyth Kingsway First School

Kathryn Bassam, Blyth Kingsway First School

Schools in Seaton Valley will be the first to go Comprehensive in September 1969 [*June 1968*]

Eleven Plus.

The 'Eleven-plus' exam was coming up and Ben's father arranged an interview with Mr Hince the tall, austere headmaster. He wanted to know if there was any possibility of his son passing.

"Ben is a bright boy and he certainly stands a good chance, but I know of other youngsters who are getting private tuition."

Mr Hince knew that there were very few working class families in Seaton Delaval who could afford to keep their children at Grammar School. Most children, however clever, left school as soon as possible so they could start earning and help towards the family budget.

Ben's father was aware of the importance of the exam and it was no surprise when the result showed that the top places had been filled by children with 'professional' parents. Ben had been in the top ten but as there were very few vacant places in Blyth Grammar he was obliged to attend the 'A' stream at Astley Secondary School. Ben realised his father felt disappointment but secretly he was relieved to be going back to school with his friends from Blyth Street.

Tom Humphrey Seaton Sluice

Blyth's four day Careers and Hobbies Exhibition at Blyth Grammar School was opened by Kenneth Horne the famous TV and Radio star. [*April 1957*]

Queues lengthen at unemployment exchanges due to the predicted recession and increased number of school leavers. The 'bulge' has truly arrived. [*August 1962*]

1960

My father was a teacher at Blyth Grammar when he was appointed headmaster of a Whitley Bay secondary school. We moved down the coast but I continued my education in Blyth. Each morning the train would leave the coastal loop [now the Metro circuit] at Monkseaton and head for Blyth. On the way the train would fill up with grammar school pupils from Holywell, New Hartley and Seaton Sluice. Most of us got off at Newsham station and walked the half a mile or so down Plessey Road. The school population came from as far afield as Ashington and Newbiggin.

David Phillipson Tynemouth

Open Plan

Later in my career I taught at Tynedale Middle School but by then teaching styles had changed and there was more pressure for an open-plan approach. The school was 'purpose built' with light screens dividing the teaching 'bays' and it had none of the advantages of the self-contained solid brick classrooms of the older buildings. Inevitably there was more noise, and lack of corridors meant that visitors wishing to reach the far end of the school had to walk through, and interrupt, several classes. The classrooms, or in some cases alcoves, had floor to ceiling windows, which apart from distracting the pupils, made the classrooms unbearably hot in summer and bitterly cold in winter. The architects clearly did not consult teachers; we said the school was purpose built to drive us mad!

Jean Reid Blyth

Work began on a no-classroom school at Malvin's Close, Blyth. [*April 1971*]

Rose-Bay Willow Herb

In 1973 I began teaching at Malvin's Close First School in Blyth. It was a new purpose-built, open plan school to capture the child-centred mood of the period. I was a mature student fresh from college and also the first male class teacher in the county to work in a primary school. It was quite daunting to find myself facing thirty-five enthusiastic eight-year-olds on that first morning.

I made it through to lunchtime and in the afternoon I decided to visit the adjoining wasteground for an environmental studies lesson, as I had noticed that the area was full of the wild flower, rose-bay willow herb. It was a magnificent display with the pink petals and spindly seed pods at their September best. What an opportunity for a 'hands-on' nature study session. There were so many clumps that I allowed the children to pick one for close scrutiny and observational drawing. Several picked bunches, but that was OK, there were plenty. Back in the classroom they sat at their desks grasping the flowers and hanging onto my words as I told them how each of the small pods contained hundreds of feathery spores that could be carried on the wind to reproduce this wild plant. They were so attentive.. teaching was wonderful.

It was Gary who broke the spell (it is always a Gary or a Darren). He had made a discovery. "Hey Look!" he shouted. The class turned to Gary and watched as he shook his bunch above his head. There were squeals of delight as Gary released a thick white cloud of floating seeds. There was a stunned pause and before I could draw breath there was a spontaneous joyful outburst. Thirty-five hands were shaking their plants and millions of those damned feathery spores filled the classroom. It was as though a snowstorm had descended; the air was white and I couldn't see the children. I yelled at them to stop and eventually got through. They sat a their tables in silence holding their weedy remains. I was speechless as I watched the last o the seeds float onto the children's heads and clothes. Worst of all was the white layer tha covered the school's new cord carpet. How could I explain that to the caretaker?

The class was now very quiet, the horror at what they had done had struck home. A chil sneezed and a puffy cloud rose into the atmosphere and fell again. I was frantically wonderin how I could minimise the damage when I glanced through the floor-to-ceiling windows; m humiliation was complete. Across the courtyard, in class two, all the children and their teache had their noses up against the glass and were staring into our room with expressions of utte disbelief. Word of my disaster spread like seeds on the wind! Even now, twenty years on, if meet my older colleagues they are likely to ask:

"Do you still teach nature study?"

I'm not sure how much the kids got out of that session but I know for certain, one very ra young teacher learnt a valuable lesson. To this day, the sight of rose-bay willow herb bring out beads of perspiration on my forehead.

Andy Griffin Blyth

Malvin's Close First School Staff 1973

DOWN BY THE RIVERSIDE...

A BEAUTIFUL SUNNY FRIDAY EVENING

A beautiful
sunny
Friday
evening.

Cycling along
Blyth's
wooden pier,
sightseeing.

The start of
the summer holidays.
Calm water
promising for fisherman.

Pausing,
absorbing the salt air,
looking towards
the sharp clear
horizon.

Suddenly
from out of the
sea's dark depths,
a gleaming
salmon
leapt.

With a flash of
silver
it returned,
to chase the sprats
and seek out
sand eels.

But that moment,
that graceful
shining
arching moment,
is fixed
forever
in a childhood
memory.

Alan Mullin
Ashington

Three Blyth fishermen struggled unsuccessfully to land a thirty foot basking shark which was entangled in their nets. [*September 1960*]
84 degrees F. The warm weather had attracted jellyfish to the coast and they have already stung twenty sun-worshippers. [*August 1975*]

A monster sun-fish ten feet in length [3m] and weighing 77 pounds was caught by two youngsters off Blyth beach. [*August 1980*]

River Visit 1996

Children of Blyth Kingsway First School

There were lots of boats. I saw a dredger called Crofton. It was going upstream to get mud from beside the power station to keep the river at the right level. When it was full it would dump the mud out to sea. In the olden days, quite a long time ago, the boats used to come in and get coal and go out to lots of different places. They went south to London.

Gary Latty age 8

We all had to sketch the windmills (they had steps at the side).

We saw a man fishing at the river's edge.

There was a small boat polluting the air with diesel.

On the other side there was the wooden staithes and piers. We could not walk there because there was a sign saying it was dangerous.

Some of the windmills were turning fast, some more slowly. The white windmills each had a power box at the top and all nine had three white blades.

On the way back we passed on old lighthouse in a back street. That is tall and white as well but it isn't used now.

Keely Richardson age 8

The Lighthouse, Blyth

We sat on the kerb and sketched the power station. It had lots of windows and four big, green chimneys. Next to it was a tall crane. We watched boats come in and out. When we drew the nine white windmills we saw people fishing. On the walk back to school we passed the park and Mrs Snowden's house.

Alison Moody age 8

Mr Davison told us that in the power station there were some little pipes that were very important. There was this big room and it had lots of steam and if the steam didn't come out of the pipes then it would blow up. The pipes are there to keep the temperature right.

There was a boat on the river but it was too far down so I could not read its name. But there was a pipe coming from it and it was smoking and polluting the air and dropping oil or chemicals onto the water.

Lisa Dodds age 8

Power Station Drawing, by Lee Renfree

My friend Daniel has been up a windmill. He has also been inside the power station.

When we were sketching I was excited and a little shaky.

I saw lots of seagulls and men fishing.

Across the river some workmen were cutting down the dirty old staithes.

I took some photos.

All of our class was there but it was still calm and quiet.

Georgina Robson age 8

When we arrived it was still and quiet.

There was smoke coming out of two tall chimneys. The windmills were going around quickly. It was lovely when the sun caught them and they shone brightly.

We could see the riverbank on the other side. It was muddy and dirty and the water looked very murky.

Some of the staithes are still there where the seamen used to get their boats near the side of the river so that they could load the coal in.

It was an exciting walk.

Danielle Robinson age 8

County Council Buildings, Blyth

On the way to the harbour we stopped to look at the police station.

I sketched the big blue crane.

Suddenly the Crofton ship came by, spilling oil and polluting the river.

We looked at the big orange hoppers and drew the white windmills.

On the banks all the mud was slimy.

We saw the staithes. They are made of big blocks of brown wood.

In the old days Blyth was a very busy place with ships coming in and out all day long.

Darren White age 8

Remains of the Staithes 1996

Mr Don Kent, general manager of Blyth Harbour Commission, was awarded the OBE in the New Year's Honours List. [*January 1983*]

North & West Quays – South Harbour – 1958 (Discharging pit props)

STICK AROUND TOMMY ROBERTSON

Dark wind across
the snakes and ladders
of the empty slipway

clash of buffer to buffer
across the shunting
yards

Anorexic silhouette of
the coal staithes
against the falling sun

restlessness in the beds
of widows and men laid off

In the new dawn
twisting dove white towers
giant's teeth along
the harbour wall

harvest of the past
carried on the forever
wind,

Stick around Tommy Robertson
the future will rise
with your
memories and laughter.

Roger McDonald Holywell

The Royal Northumberland Yacht Club headquarters sank in Blyth Harbour during a gale. [*December 1949*]
A flotilla of yachts, including the new lifeboat 'Shoreline' greets round-the-world yachtsman David Scott Cowper as he sails into Blyth Harbour. His 272 day voyage broke the record by 23 days and fellow members of the Royal Northumberland Yacht Club gave him a warm welcome. [*May 1980*]

BLYTH WIND FARM

Strong are they at harbour edge
Bodies made of steel
Who lift their arms unto the wind
And use them as a wheel.

To harvest all their strength
That comes from sea-blown gales
They stand erect and picturesque
Dressed in their windmill flails

Audrey Barton Blyth

The crew of five from the tug Chipchase were dramatically rescued from the river after the vessel overturned and sank near Blyth Shipyard. [*July 1964*]

Blyth lifeboat coxswain Charlie Hatcher, was presented with a RNLI bronze bravery medal for his part in rescuing three men, five minutes before their fishing boat sank. [*May 1983*]

A COASTAL VIEW

[From Seaton Sluice promontory]

Bobbing boats in a peaceful harbour,
A contrast to the wild awesome sea.
Foaming arches breaking on the sandy shore
Frantically beating against the rocks
Echoing a great rage with its clamour;
A greyish-green uneasy sea
Filling the air with its tangy salty smell.
St Mary's lighthouse gleams beyond the headland
Whilst whirring windmills compensate
For ugly chimneys which mar the horizon.
A grim reminder of the need for power;
Yet the might of the sea is all encompassing.

Pamela Mahan Seaton Sluice

Firemen lowered hot acetylene oxygen cylinders into the river as they were 'liable to blow up like bombs' following a fire in the blacksmiths at Blyth quayside. [*October 1955*]

Ships from ten different European countries sailed in and out of Blyth Port carrying mining timber, cement, roof tiles and other essential goods, and, according to the Port Medical Officer, they left behind 86 black rats. [*May 1955*]

Seaside

I love to go to the seaside on a Sunday with my Grandma and Granda. We go to Blyth beach and sometimes I take a friend and we go in the water to look for jellyfish. Occasionally we go to St Mary's Lighthouse but I like the beach better because the sand is nice and soft to run along and race with my friend. If there are pebbles we look for 'skimmers' and see who can get the furthest.

Blyth Beach 1960

I also like to hear the sea bash against the cliffs and I love to smell the salty sea air.

If the tide is up, we just sit in the car and watch the waves, but that is boring. Although I like to watch the seagulls float on the sea (we always wonder how they do it) or swoop down to catch a fish.

I recommend the beach to old people because it is quiet and not too noisy. But keep away from the town where the drunks are (this is Whitley Bay).

Emma Gilmore (Age 12)

St Peter's Middle School, Cramlington

HUMFORD WOODS

Humford Woods is a lovely place
Where people walk with gentle pace.
Flowers bloom throughout the year
Foxgloves, orchids - they're all there.

Thrushes, wrens and coots are heard
But the blue-tit is my favourite bird.
It's not his whistle or the way he flies
But there's something about his beady eyes;
Perched above in the highest tree
He turns his head and looks at me.

I love the smell of the riverbank air
And there's teeming fish if you stop and stare.
Spring and summer's really good
When the wildlife thrives in this lush green wood.

Steven Alexander Age 13
Brockwell Middle School
Cramlington

To The Woods

East Hartford School Visit 1995

I was playing with Michael by the stepping stones and he shouted to Gavin

"I've caught a big fish!"

It was about five centimetres long.

Gavin came rushing up with his jar

and we kept the net in the water until he came.

Then we tipped the fish in gently and watched it swim about.

We didn't think it was very happy.

Later on we let it go after we had had a good look at it.

It had bits of gold and black but mostly it was grey.

If you're a fish there's a lot of danger.

Steven Cherry Age 9

I caught some fish in my net beside the stepping stones at Humford Woods. There was two of them. They were grey and spotty but silver underneath. I watched them swimming for ages in the glass jar then I gave them to a little girl and she put them in her yellow bucket. Afterwards she went for a walk so I let them go in a shadowy place. Fish are wild and they might have a mam or dad.

Kirby Brough Age 9

There were lots of flies in Humford woods.

It was nice and sunny and they were all around our heads.

I was trying to slap them away but they kept coming back.

I think they thought we were big flowers.

Malcolm Stemp Age 9

I put my net in the water and looked very closely.

There were lots of tiny fish next to the reeds.

I scooped some up in the net
and the little silvery fish were wriggling.

Very carefully I patted them into a jar
and when they plopped into the clear water
they flicked and flashed around.

Gavin Thow Age 9

I took my shoes and socks off and I stepped in the paddling pool.

Michael said:

"I bet you can't do this."

Michael jumped in with his eyes closed and he didn't fall down.

I got out and tried to jump in with my eyes closed but slipped with all my clothes on.

I was soaked and I didn't have a change.

All my clothes were sticking to me

But I was still happy.

Richard Park Age 9

The Finn-Heide, a paper-carrying ship, docked at Blyth Harbour and became the first of a new traffic to the port. [*September 1969*]

The Corona, the biggest ship ever to enter Blyth Harbour at 19,163 tons, arrived with a cargo of alumina for the new Alcan plant. [*October 1971*]

The Long Jump

Starlight Castle in Holywell Dene   Tom Allan Collection

It was during the Olympic year of 1954 when me and Baz and Keith went to Holywell Dene. Baz was a tall, willowy lad who was the school high-jump champion. We had gone to the dene to explore and we were on the Whitley Bay side of the river near the farm. The stream was narrow there, if you could call it a stream. The tide was out and there was just a thin trickle of water running down the centre of what was really an expanse of black coal-thickened mud. Even then I could never work out how a beautiful spot like Holywell Dene could have such a filthy river running through it.

From where we stood there was about a dozen feet [4m] to the other side of the bank and that gap held Baz's attention. It might have been the summer sun, or watching newsreels of the Melbourne Olympics, or simply Baz being too big for his boots. Whatever it was, he was determined:

"I could jump that."

We told him it was a daft idea but he just kept staring at the black gulf in front of him. He wouldn't listen, the more we argued the more stubborn he became. He started stepping out a run-up away from the bank. It took him ages. He was showing off as well, pretending to be a long-jumper as he wandered to the water's edge and looking at the point on the other bank where he expected to land. We were getting bored because we still thought he'd dip out. Keith told him so and that seemed to trigger something off because the next moment he was up and running. He raced to the edge, slammed his foot into the verge and took off.

It was a tremendous effort. Baz sailed through the air.. but it wasn't quite good enough. It was like a cartoon where one of the characters hangs in mid-air over a cliff before plummeting. For a moment, and I can still vividly recall it, he seemed suspended, then a split second later there was a perfect outline of his shape in the fresh mud below.

It was quite scary at first because he disappeared but then Baz surfaced chest deep in the stuff. It was thick and clinging. We watched him silently, almost mesmerised, as he waded across the last few feet to the other side. It was Keith who said:

"Come on, over the bridge."

We had to run a fair distance before we could meet up with Baz and he was just standing there, covered. It was impossible to read any expression into his face but he was obviously miserable.

Keith suggested we go to the farm for help. We knocked on the door and a horrified woman told us to get ourselves away home. We'd only wanted to clean him up. We tried to get the thick off with twigs and leaves but that just smeared it in.

We walked Baz to Wakenshaw's shop next to the Delaval Arms. The woman behind the counter was kinder but it was the same message "Get yourselves away home as quick as you can."

That meant a bus journey. We got on the bus alright and luckily the conductor was at the far end taking fares otherwise I'm sure he wouldn't have let us on. When he saw us he shouted:

"Keep off them seats!"

We stood in the aisles and as people squeezed past they looked at Baz as if he was muck, which I suppose he was! He had a struggle getting the money out of his back pocket and I could see how unhappy he was because there was two white streams running down his cheeks. Baz was a hard lad, he never usually cried.

When we walked home, or in Baz's case waddled, I noticed the mud was cracking as it was drying, even though poor Baz was shivering. We'd hardly spoken to each other. Keith and I were too embarrassed; it was like walking alongside the creature from the black lagoon. We left him at his back gate and then ran behind a shed to see what happened.

He called out pathetically "Mam!" and she came to the door. I didn't think she would take her son into her arms but I did think she might be sympathetic. Some hope! He got such a mouthful. She would have clipped him if he hadn't been so filthy. We saw her go in and leave Baz on the doorstep. Soon his granda followed his mam out and he had some choice words as well. We were sorry for Baz, but we felt even sorrier when his granda got the hose pipe out. Baz had to take off his shirt and shorts and shoes and socks. He was in his underpants when his granda washed him down with icy water. Baz turned white once again. We could hear him bawling when his granda had finished.. and it was then, when he was clean, that his mam clouted him. That's when we ran home.

Years later I met Baz in a pub and we talked about old times. I mentioned the 'jump' and realised it was the first time any of us had spoken about it. It had been such a harrowing experience for the three 11 year olds. Baz remembered the incident and we were both convulsed as we went through every detail. It was as though we had stored up all our laughter for this one moment. My jaws ached for two days after.

East Hartford and Humford Mill Footpath

Bill Blyth

THERE WERE SHIPS...

The Shipyards

Blyth Shipyard was situated between the bus station and the Golden Fleece pub at the ferry landing and behind the high wall along Regent Street. That small patch of land was occupied by a 1500 skilled workforce. Shipbuilding had taken place there since the early 1700's and many Blyth families supplied generations of craftsmen.

The boilermakers were the elite as far as I was concerned with the platers on the top of the ladder. Our view was that the other trades had a servicing role. The platers' 'helpers' were superior labourers and at the bottom of the pile were the apprentices, which is where I began at the age of sixteen.

It was a hard physical job, open to the elements, and as you would expect working by the river, very damp. The high skeleton-like ribs of the ships could be seen soaring over the road. There was never enough room, you always seemed to be cramped in the confined spaces. We often had to wheel the heavy steel plates on a very long-handled iron wheeled bogie. This was pulled and manhandled by the platers' helpers who went by the name of 'humpers', for obvious reasons. We had to manoeuvre it in the narrow passage ways and if we caught anybody's ankle we got to know about it.

We worked from 7:30am to 12 noon, had lunch, then came back at one o'clock to finish the shift at 5 pm; an eight and a half hour day. People would avoid York Street at the end of the shift because when the buzzer went, 1500 men would burst through the gates into Regent Street. It was quite a sight with hundreds of bikes spilling out onto the road and stopping all oncoming traffic. Amazingly, in less than four minutes, the area would be completely clear. Nobody stayed behind!

As an appreciation of the efforts of Blyth Shipyard employees for rushing the 'William G Walkley' to completion, the men were given a bottle of beer and a sandwich each. [*June 1953*]

Blyth from the Air

The platers were very highly skilled. It was an education just watching them in action. In ships there were plenty of curves so the inch-and-a-half [4cm] thick sheets of steel had to be cut to size and shaped to fit the contours of the hull. These craftsmen would run a length of thin plater's chalk line (like fine string) through a piece of ordinary soft chalk then apply it to marks onto steel plates which could be twenty feet in length. With a deft flick of the wrist they would whip a perfect curve onto the surface of the plates. They called it 'throwing the line'. It was always accurate; their 'eye' was uncanny. They had been on the job so long it was like working on instinct.

One old plater was so proud and protective that if you asked him how he did things he'd say "I'm not telling you." His attitude was, that what he'd picked up, he'd found out for himself by trial and error and he believed that was the best way to learn. The miserable old sod!

I can recall some terrible winters when you just had to touch the sheet metal and if you were not careful your fingers could stick to them; they were that cold. One of my early jobs was to melt the ice with a burner's torch and then cover it with sawdust to dry them off. All this had to be done before the plater could start 'marking off'.

The plates were very heavy and the platers who did the shearing and punching had to guide them into the cutting shears along the chalk lines or under the belt-driven machines that punched rivet holes in the plates. They had to nudge them with their stomachs which were only protected by a rough and ready tarpaulin cover or more likely a makeshift sack apron. The plates were then positioned by crane onto the ribs of the hull and rivets would hold them into place - there was no margin for error. If the holes were out of line it would slow the platers up. They did the erecting and since it was all piece work anyone who held the job up was not very popular.

Most of the platers were either heavily built and muscular or they were thin and angular. I can only remember three who were obese and they were well past their prime. Among the ranks of platers were two former professional footballers; one had been on Celtic's books. Two were local rugby players, four were well-known sprinters and there was a cyclist who rode for miles every week-end. It was said he invented cyclo-cross. Many were very good ballroom dancers. They were so light on their feet, no doubt due to the hard exercise they went through every day. Hence the popularity of the Roxy Ballroom.

The noise was indescribable. Practically everybody who worked in the yard suffered from deafness. The lads working the punches had no ear muffs or protection. If you wanted to speak to anyone on the job you had a strange way of communicating; you talked sideways on! We would stand cheek to cheek and I would bellow instructions in my mate's right ear and he would yell back into my right ear.

With the pneumatic tools and constant vibration the men had white finger ends and suffered a painful ailment known as Reynard's Phenomena. It was a circulatory problem which affected them later in life. It is hard to imagine the conditions that were worked in those days and with hindsight you wonder why they put up with it. The safety aspect was non-existent; nobody was supplied with hard hats. The only protection was the cloth cap which every man wore. When working with a welder they only gave you one glove, left or right, to protect your hands from the red hot sparks that flew around when you were holding the jobs in place. When complained, the management just shrugged their shoulders. I kicked up a fuss and exposed the stupidity of their rule and eventually they gave me a glove for each hand. That was breakthrough at the time.

The welding caused problems with the eyes. You were provided with tinted goggles but you couldn't see the chalk marks through them. I had to line up smaller jobs with one hand for tack or spot welding, then try to cover my eyes and face with my other hand before calling "Now!". My tack-welder mate would weld the job but more often than not I got the full force of the flash. That would make my eyes water and I couldn't stop them. It could be embarrassing. I was in the pictures once and even in the dark they started to stream. It must have been a sad picture because when the lights came up this old woman sitting next to me said "Never mind son.. here's a sweetie."

The reading of the commissioning order for the mine hunter Stripe. Ceremony at Import Dock, Blyth Sept. 196

I was a regular client at the ambulance room suffering from conjunctivitis and ray burn. No wonder I wear spectacles today!

Before 1960 nobody knew, or was told, about the dangers of asbestos. I remember how they used to line the engine room with sheets of the stuff and the joiners would cut it to size with their hand saws. There would be loads of this lethal white dust lying around and it would cling to your clothes. Many's the time I've seen the lads have 'snowball' fights because you could roll it up into compact balls. I'd often been working below decks when someone would drop an asbestos bomb onto my head for a joke. It would cover you all over and you would be taking the stuff home on your overalls. In later years I found out that I could have been contaminating the rest of the household.

I knew one lad who worked at the yards, six-foot-six he was.. a big strong, strapping bloke. I met him three years ago at Blyth when he was paying his poll tax. I didn't recognise him. He was small, wizened and both his lungs were shot; his gullet had gone too. He couldn't swallow, he was just wasting away. He must have known, but he was still cheerful. Three months later I heard he'd died.. that was asbestosis.

They were a hard breed of men but in some ways they were their own worst enemies. Men didn't complain about their lot; they were tough and proved it every day by performing in this hard physical environment. I actually saw a man with a thin piece of steel, shaped like an axe blade, sticking out of his head. It had been dropped from a great height and embedded itself into this bloke's skull - through his cloth cap. I watched the blood pour down his face, into his ears and over his collar but he just calmly walked to First Aid where they immediately phoned for an ambulance to take him to hospital.

It was very rare for a shipyard worker to have all their fingers intact. One way or another they lost them on the job and this was especially true of the platers who were the punchers and shearers. I remember one lad who was working on the guillotine. I had been eating my bait with him and we'd been having a laugh. When I restarted work, word came round that there had been an accident in the plater's shed. It was my mate, he'd lost all the finger ends of one hand. There had been oil on the brake drum and the guillotine blade had come back down when he was retrieving the job. I felt sick inside that day but within weeks he was back doing the same work shoving the plates with the palm of his hand!

Bad as it was, it didn't compare to the fellers who used to build ships 20 years earlier. To hear the old guys talking about the way they riveted these ships was fascinating. All the ships had 'double bottoms' which means they built another floor in the bowels of the boat. There was usually an 18 inch gap [45cm] of framework in between. Men crawled into the cavities to rivet the steel floor into place. What a job that must have been.

Riveters worked in teams or squads. In the team a 'heater' had to take the rivets, usually about three to four inches long and an inch in diameter, and heat them until they were almost white-hot in a coal fire. Then, with tongs, he threw the rivet to a 'catcher' who caught it in a metal bucket. The catcher pushed it through the holes which joined the plates to the frame and a 'holder-up' supported it from below with a protective cup and used his body as a buttress. Above, two riveters would simultaneously strike the rivets 'whilst the iron was hot' and flatten it, top and bottom. This was how they worked out in the open yard and the same method was

Blyth Shipyard Riveting Squad 1939.
(left to right)
Tom Rochester (holder up)
Robert Buckham (left hander)
James William Cole (right hander)

applied in the confined space within the bowels of the vessel with candles as the only source of light - and you hear miners talk about hard working conditions! One of the old fellers told me about this mate of his who had a nasty accident. He was a holder-up and was working in the double bottom darkness, where speed was essential. On this particular day, the white hot rivet had been thrown and he pointed to the catcher where he wanted it putting: "In there!" he shouted, and pushed his finger through the hole they were about to rivet.. you've guessed it. It was dark wasn't it? The riveters on the other side hit and mashed his finger with their hammers!

They built some magnificent ships at Blyth as they had done for nearly 200 years. The Caxton was the last of the riveted ships to be built and that was as late as the 1950's.

Blyth Shipyard repaired them as well; and that was often a terrible job. Can you imagine getting into the bottom of a collier filled with London mud and having to clean it all out for repairing? They were foisty-smelling and full of orange coloured filth. You had to go into the holes with your portable light and sort it out.

Eddie Cain Blyth

BLYTH SHIPYARDS TO CLOSE. The news was broken whilst 1200 workers were on their annual holiday. [*August 1966*]

It was a huge loss to the town when it closed. The yard was on its fortnight holiday and I had just had a successful interview with the Evening Chronicle to work in the photography department at Thomson House in Newcastle. I was actually writing out my notice when I heard it on the 6 o'clock news. I stopped with the pen in my hand, I could not believe it. I was stunned, and I think that sums up the reaction of most of the people I spoke to. It was total disbelief. After the initial numbness the workers were angry and upset. The owners were Dutch and it was difficult for the men to air their grievances. One lad wrote to them and his reply came back from the head office in Hong Kong! So who could the men complain to in Blyth?

Keith Thompson Cramlington

Shipyard Unions on the Blyth and Tyne threaten to call out 70,000 on a token strike to protest against lack of action in high quarters to save Blyth Shipyard. [*November 1966*]

The last vessel to be built by Blyth Dry Docks and Shipping Co Ltd. was launched by shop steward Charles Long. [*November 1966*]

The Docks. Blyth

Pacific Princess (22,000 tons) Ready for launching at Blyth Shipyards. June 1964

In 1966 I was making £33.00 a week and that was good money. The yard was still doing piece work then, and that was a healthy sign. So naturally when the closure announcement came it was hard to accept. On the day England were beating Germany in the final of the World Cup, the managers were called in for a meeting, and that was it. Closed! Perfect timing. The men were out on their annual holidays and the following Monday there was a meeting in Blyth Market. It was a dreadful time. The workers were intelligent and sharp-witted but on that day they were completely at a loss. No-one could tell them why the yard had shut-down. Nobody knew anything. The men just wandered around in utter bewilderment. My uncle who was the shop steward could tell them nothing then, although he promised he would find out and keep them informed.. he was as good as his word in the forthcoming weeks.

To wind down the yard and finish off the orders, a handful were kept on but week by week more would be laid off. Every Friday we would see them coming round with the dreaded brown envelope - like the black spot. It got so that you felt guilty if your mate was finished and you were kept on. There was no bitterness amongst the workers towards each other it was just a feeling of sadness and regret. And even at this time there could be a funny side. One of the yard carpenters applied for a job as a bus conductor and he said at the time, "It's better than travelling to work."

Many of the lads, including myself, found work at Wallsend but it wasn't the same. I'd been on the Tyne nine years when one of the lads I worked with said he thought I was from Sunderland. Blyth Shipyard was an extended family. Everyone knew each other and the bond that came from working with townsfolk produced a pride and loyalty that was to create some of the finest ships ever to sail on the seven seas.

Eddie Cain Blyth

The largest ever product of the town's shipyard to date, 19,000 ton oil tanker 'Blyth Adventurer' was launched [*September 1957*]

The 23,000 ton Chapel River, the biggest ship ever to be built at Blyth, was launched. [*May 1962*]

Shaun Robinson

Blyth Harbour Drawing by Shaun Robinson

Industrial Photography

I was always keen on photography and when I was eighteen I worked in Blyth shipyards as an industrial photographer. It was interesting and unusual work. There was two of us and one of our jobs was to take X-ray pictures of stress points on the ships so that we could pick up any possible structural weaknesses. The ship's specification demanded that up to thirty photographs should be taken. The stress point could be at a cross-junction of four steel plates or under the bow of the ship; they were usually awkward to get at. It wasn't like taking a snapshot either. This was in the mid-1960s and looking back it was quite a hazardous job because we were dealing with highly dangerous radioactive material. My mate George and I were always given a wide berth as we pulled our 'yellow bomb' through the yard on its trolley. The 'bomb' was the lead case which held the isotope rod that produced the X-ray pictures. It was about the size of a pencil and it was effective for up to four months. When it was changed a fresh isotope had to be put into the case using tongs that were about twelve feet long - even that was too close. George was impatient and if he was around he would just pick it up with his fingers and swop it over in a couple of seconds. He reckoned that by fiddling about with the tongs for ten minutes there was more risk of contamination.

It was considered so dangerous that we worked on a Saturday morning when the men were not on overtime and we had the yard to ourselves with only a single foolhardy labourer. He was well-paid and would fetch and carry or test the scaffolding which could be 40-50 feet off the ground. He did this by jumping up and down on it! On a typical Saturday we would fix a large photographic plate to the stress point on the inside of the hull and then, this was the tricky part, we would go outside the ship and line up the isotope. Once in position, we had to carefully remove the lid of the lead container (above your head) and expose the plate. It would take about twenty minutes for the radiation to penetrate the metal's thickness and give an image. It was time-consuming and we were doing well if we could manage three in a morning. We could be working in cramped, confined spaces such as the notorious double-bottoms of the ships, and part of the problem was that you could not see, smell, or taste the radiation. We did have a sensitive badge that we pinned to our breast pocket to monitor the radiation dosage and we were sent to the hospital for regular blood checks.

There was once quite a scare when our labourer recorded an excessively high dose of radiation. He had dropped his badge onto the scaffolding when a photograph was being exposed and he clambered down to retrieve it then put it back on. He was rushed to the hospital and detained after that incident but his blood count was actually low due to a heavy cold.

All the plates were developed in a darkroom on the site and the results were mostly OK. However if an X-ray showed dark patches along the joints where the plates had been welded or caulked then there was an enquiry. Dark areas meant a bad weld and impurities (the polite word) in the joint which could be dirt, grit, or even a cigarette end! The men were on piece work and it took a lot to slow them down. The foreman plater, the foreman fitter, and the manager would examine the X-rays and make a decision. They might want other X-ray photographs for confirmation or have the welding done again. There was no cutting corners or allowing shoddy work to get through. I read recently of a ship that broke in half and twenty or so lives were lost. Shipbuilding brings with it a huge responsibility and it must be terrible to live with the knowledge that your skills (or lack of them) had led to even a single death. It was like that in the Blyth yard; there was a team of men that took enormous pride in their work.

Keith Thompson Cramlington

Hughes Bolckow Shipbuilders secured three Admiralty destroyers for demolition: Montrose, Antelope and the Warrior. [*August 1946*]

A 16,000 ton former Cunard liner the 'Alaunia' sailed into Blyth Harbour to be broken up [*September 1957*]

Hughes Bolckow

Across the river from Blyth Shipyard lay Battleship Wharf, the official name of Hughes Bolckow Ltd, shipbreakers. Ships of every shape and size, from all over the world, made their final journey up the River Blyth. All usable metal was recycled and the railway nearby gave direct access to Consett Steelworks. But it was not just the ship's superstructure that was re-usable, the fittings and furnishings, often from Cunard liners, were equally valuable. Many a municipal building, Masonic hall or pub, has benefited from a Bolckow auction. The joinery workshop attached to the breakers yard also produced high quality garden furniture from the reclaimed timber which they sold by mail order. In the grounds of the Palace of Westminster, Blyth craftsmen produced the benches at this seat of power.

Bolckows was a hard physical environment like its shipyard neighbours opposite yet there was still a sense of pride in their work. The management, conscious of the recycling process maintained:

'Battleship Wharf is no graveyard for ships of yesterday; it is rather the birthplace of ships of tomorrow.'

Sam Lovey, a foreman for many years, recollects:

Shipbreaking before the war (1918) was an affair of hammer and chisel. Ships were broken up by 'unbuttoning'; in other words dismantling was the reverse of their assembly. In the early days the men ran a diamond point along a chalked line then chiselled out a grooved line. It was then turned over, bolstered and hammered away until it broke in two. You had to be careful when you broke up cast iron. We would place the scrap in a deep pit and drop a heavy ball onto it but it could shoot off in all directions.

It was 10-hour day with top rate 7d [3p an hour]. During the war [WW1] when most skilled men had been called up, we recruited women and invalid soldiers. The women proved tougher than some of the men. They cleaned out the ship's bilges, jacked out the nails from the decking and helped manhandle the scrap into the railway wagons. When we were dismantling a schooner in 1916 I wanted somebody to climb up the mast with me to hold my tools. There was a gale wind blowing and the only volunteer was a woman, Margaret Stafford; she went aloft in a skip. A few years later we were married.

One time my wife was working below decks in a wooden barque when she found what she thought was a fur rug, just the thing for our front room. She went to pick it up and it dissolved into dozens of shiny black rats. They had been packed nose-to-tail so tightly that in the half darkness they gave the appearance of a rug.

[Extract from 'Battleship Wharf' 1960 by Horace White. A history of shipbreaking on the River Blyth]

Hughes Bolckow Shipbuilders secured three Admiralty destroyers for demolition: Montrose, Antelope and the Warrior. [*August 1946*]

A 16,000 ton former Cunard liner the 'Alaunia' sailed into Blyth Harbour to be broken up [*September 1957*]

Fish Quay Blyth.

The Royal Northumberland Yacht Club on today's river

Shipyard Animals

Luckily at Blyth Shipyard, rats were few and far between, although you could find them (if you were looking) under the old plater's shed. This shed had a heavy wooden floor that was used for marking out jobs before transferring them to the steel plates. The floor was about a foot [30cm] off the ground and packed underneath with rubbish and debris from the generations who had used it. On one occasion a crane driver was in there cleaning his hands with a ball of paraffin-soaked waste when he spotted a rat. Quick as a flash, he lit the waste, and threw it. Amazingly, the blazing ball landed on the creature's back, and stuck there! In total fear it ran under the floorboards and set fire to all the accumulated debris. It was sheer pandemonium. They had to call the fire brigade to put the blaze out and it took days to clear away all the rubbish. The crane driver's part in the incident was quietly hushed up.

Maybe the reason for the shortage of rats in the yard was the abundance of cats. There was one cat in particular that used to sleep near the furnace for warmth. The furnace heated the fifty foot long [15m] bars of steel that were used for the ship's frame and they were pulled in and out by an electric winch and steel hawser. On this particular day, the sleeping cat suddenly woke up with a start and jumped, four square, straight onto the white-hot frame that was being removed. With an almighty screech, the cat flew about twenty feet into the air before landing on its badly burned paws. A well-meaning plater's helper grabbed it and thrust it into the oil tank. Sadly, that did no good and the cat died in agony. Still, the furnace came in handy - it doubled as a crematorium.

Eddie Cain Blyth

River Blyth 1996

The first ship since 1966 was launched at Blyth when a £1m stern freezer trawler took to the river. The 250 ft [80 meters] 'factory ship' was built by Gregsons. [*November 1972*]

IN THE STORE...

Deliveries

My first proper job was as a delivery boy for Thompson Stores near the marketplace. A ship had docked, I think it was called the Ballarat, and it had a very friendly Irish crew. They had placed a 'shipping order' of over a £100 and when it was complete it filled about 20 egg-boxes. My job was to deliver them all by grocery bike to the ship which happened to be docked on the other side of the river. I had to cross by the chain ferry and since I could only take two boxes at a time that meant ten journeys! I remember starting out at first light when the tide was low but by the time I had finished the tide was at its highest and swelling.

It was getting dark when I completed the trip and crew must have been impressed with my effort because they had had a whip-round. I was amazed when the captain said "Will ten pounds do you?" Would it do? I was only on £4-9-6d [£4.50p] a week; this was more than twice my wages!

These generous Irishmen poured silver and copper from their hat into my two open hands. was overwhelmed as I left the ship. I don't know if it was the swell of the sea, the semi darkness, or just me walking on air, but I tripped on the gangplank and fell headlong onto the boards. The money flew out of my hands and into the black waters below. It was a moment that is imprinted on my mind forever. I can still vividly remember watching the last penny roll across the plank and plop into the sea. It seemed to be the worst thing that had ever happened to me in my fifteen years. I went home so upset. We didn't have much money in the family and I was afraid that my mam might be cross. I was right to be afraid.. she was furious!

I wonder if my careful attitude towards money started that day?

Mick Davison Blyth

Thompson's Shop 1960

More than 600 shop workers protest against the Gower Report which recommends that stores should stay open longer. Workers currently work until 6pm on a 44 hour shift. [*May 1947*]

Blyth's Chamber of Trade decided that the townspeople did not want later shopping hours. [*September 1952*]

Only a week before it was due to come into effect, Blyth's plan for a 5-day shopping week fell through, chiefly because many traders decided not to support it. [*Feb. 1965*]

Broken Biscuits

After school, we would go to the grocers and ask for broken biscuits. If the woman behind the counter was in a good mood, she might wander over to the biscuits which were always kept in tins with glass lids, and angled so you could see inside. She would seek out bits and pieces from all the tins and give you maybe half a bag for penny. The lady in Walter Willson's was always kind to me, that is, until my mam found out. I saw no harm in it but my mam said it was like begging and that I was shaming the family.

My friend Baz used to open the door of the shops and shout things like:

"Have you got any broken biscuits? You should be more careful" and we'd run for it.

Stupid really.

He would go into newsagents and yell "Have you got any Wild Woodbines? You should tame them."

He went into a cake shop and got as far as:

"Have you got any cream puffs? You should.." and he got such a clout.

He hadn't seen the manager by the door. I remember asking him afterwards:

"Have you got any red ears?"

Bill Blyth

New Hartley post-master, Tom Kenny, refuses to hand over cash to armed raiders. He raised the alarm and snatched the safe keys, preventing three robbers from grabbing a massive haul.
[*October 1981*]

The Shops

My friend and I walk to the shops every Saturday morning because it's a day when we're both not doing anything.

At the shops there are different places to buy things.

We always look forward to going and I get excited because there is always something I want.

It's boring sitting around the house. Going to the shops takes the day up.
It's safer too, than hanging around the streets with nothing to do. There are different ways to get there and our younger brothers like to come as well.

We see people rushing about or just looking. We can stay for hours on end.

During the week I do jobs for my mam and dad and I sometimes get money from them. That money goes straight into my money box for the shops.

If we treat ourselves, we might go to Greggs, the cafe. That's a very popular place.

We go so many times that we know all the cheap and dear shops.

At nights when we can't go to the shops my friend and I talk about what we have bought and decide if it was a good buy or not.

There isn't a Saturday we don't go.

Marissa Glendinning (Age 11)

St Peter's Middle School,

Cramlington

Blyth's oldest and best known departmental store, Hedley Youngs, established 97 years ago, was taken over by a South Shields firm.
[*September 1959*]

Manor Walks

I go to Manor Walks shopping centre every Saturday with my friend. If we want a bite to eat we go to Greggs or McDonalds for a treat! I remember Greggs from when I was maybe three or four years old, my Mum used to buy me sausage rolls so I called it the 'sausage roll shop'. The shops are very popular and there are always lots of people around. You can buy anything from presents to sweets and it has such a good selection of shops that you never have far to go for what you want. The leisure centre is nearby so you can go for a swim or do other sporting activities.

At Christmas time it is very special. There is Santa's Grotto for the little children and the decorations are put up and Christmas music is played. The staff in the shops are friendly especially when you are looking for presents.

The most popular shops are in this range: clothes, gifts, chemists, banks and food shops. I am lucky because I only have to walk by a few cycle-tracks to get to Manor Walks.

Helen Hawkins (Age 11)

St Peter's Middle School,

Cramlington

Newsagents, Blyth

Battling Billy Wells, a well-known Blyth character and founder of the town's first taxi service, died age 63. [*February 1966*]

Blyth's heart is in it's market place
There is life
Pulse
Pace
Here is the bustling face
Of industry

Blyth is a talking town
Doorway groups discuss
Folk speak on the bus

Sidetrack to accordion strains
Manoeuvre through the crowded lanes
Blyth is a pushchair town
Full of mothers bearing down
Upon slow walkers

Tapping men with sticks
Retreat
Opt out from bustle
Take a seat
And watch the human race
Around the market place.

Audrey Barton Blyth

Arthur Sidgwick (47) had to jump for his life when his ice-cream van exploded on the Bog Houses to Hartford road. [*January 1962*]

As a result of the glorious bank holiday sunshine a refrigerator caught fire in a Waterloo Road shop [*August 1955*]

Shopping [Pre-War]

The market place in Blyth went on till about twelve o'clock at night just before the war. Dazzling bright pressure lamps lit the scene like a carnival.

There were three butchers in Croft Road at that time and for many years after. Ashby's, William Redford, and where the veterinary surgery is now, the original slatted wooden ceiling of the butchers can still be seen. Our family butcher was Redford's and I can still visualise the curved chopping block table and the counter with its weighing machine and wrapping paper. The customers stood inside on the sawdust strewn wooden floor and whole or partial carcasses hung suspended on hooks. It was so busy late on a Saturday night that I remember Mr Redford telling my mother that he would still be able to do business if he stayed open until two o'clock in the morning.

The cattle killing building was situated at the bottom of Lower Hedley Avenue (now re-named Little Hedley) and often when we played in that area we heard the loud thuds of cattle being slaughtered. This sound carried quite a distance, and equally loud was the braying of the penned animals, anticipating their fate.

Thompsons, the Red Stamp store, sold household goods (hardware) at the end of Croft Road by the arcade. This area on a Saturday night was ablaze with lamplight from the cluster of shops; there was not a dark patch to be seen. In this part of town you would often see the Musical Box Man who would stand at the side of the road churning out his tinkling Victorian melodies such as 'It's a Long Way to Tipperary', 'Goodbye Dolly Gray' and 'Tara-ra-boom-de-ay'. He turned the handle steadily and with his free hand he would signal 'Thanks' as coppers were thrown into the old pram that he used to carry his musical box.

Brian Watson Cramlington

The Youth Employment Committee say that many girls are out of work due to the delay in supplying glasses. [*October 1949*]

Dad [Extract]

Saturday afternoons when I was small are a permanent fixture in my mind. This was when my parents went to buy the Sunday joint and Dad being such a man for his food had to be in on the act. He caused Mam great embarrassment by standing outside the shop window watching as she was served. I can remember one occasion when he bolted into the shop, dragging me with him, to confront the butcher. He told him to weigh the joint again. Apparently Dad had doubts on previous shopping trips and this time he had seen for sure. The meat had been plonked onto the scale-pan and it was whipped off again before the pointer had time to settle. It caused quite a fuss but there was never any short weight after that.

With the meat safe in the bottom of the old wicker shopping basket, off we went to the market across the road. I was always a little bit nervous of the crowds pushing about there. We always met people my parents knew; sometimes Dad's workmates shopping with their wives. I usually went home richer by a copper or two given me by the older ones with no young families of their own. Dad always bought the fruit and sweets as our week-end treat at the market.

On some Saturdays when we returned home, he would get out the old black scales with the brass weights. If he was dubious as to the honesty of the fruit-seller and discovered he had been overcharged, his coat would be briskly pulled off the peg and put onto his back in record time and off he would go, back to the market to see justice done! A real Doubting Thomas, Mam said he was (his name was Tom). I can recall Dad telling the stallholder that he was not serving the customers fruit as good as what was on display. At my young age I found all this very interesting and thought Dad was very brave. I wondered why Mam turned pink and walked away. If he knew he was right nothing would move him. He became respected for this and one of the traders used to say to him "Pick your own Tom, then you'll know you've not been diddled."

There were two men who stood with boxes of comics at their feet; one in the market and one over the road near the London and Newcastle Tea Company. I used to stare at the comics; the garish colours of the of the pictures and the strong smell of the print made them seem very exciting to children. Mam disapproved strongly of "Those nasty American comics with all that slang!" Dad was boss, I was often bought one. At home I noticed they very soon disappeared.. or got lost.

These trips to the market in the winter months were even more fascinating. As it turned dark in the afternoon, the stalls all had oil-lamps burning and the reeking fumes mixed with the pleasant smell of fruit and vegetables. The lamps threw out an acid yellow glow and the hissing and popping provided a background to the cheerful banter of the stallholders and their customers. It was all such a happy, uncomplicated atmosphere. The oranges, reds, greens and yellows of the greengrocer stalls were like piled up jewels, ready to tumble onto the ground. The damp earthy smell of the potatoes mingled with that of people's coats, recently soaked by a downpour. All this was very overpowering but Dad holding my hand made me feel safe. It seemed such a long walk back home, especially for little legs. If it was particularly cold, wet or windy, Dad would open the bottom buttons of his overcoat and cover me with the lower edge as we walked up the road. I felt so warm and safe there as I listened to the muffled bump, bump of Dad's feet as we walked along.

Dorothy Redpath Blyth

Thirteen year old twins, Cedric and Lawrence Caisley, were presented with fountain pens for preventing a serious fire at the Cooperative Drapery Department on Waterloo Road, Blyth. [*March 1958*]

Fred Vincent's drapery shop in Seaton Delaval was completely gutted by fire [*Jan. 1961*]

Forty-eight members of staff at Woolworth's in Blyth (1954)

Wartime

I have vivid memories of the period when food was rationed; this was during the war and a few years after. The whisper used to get around if there were new supplies in town. My mother recalls when Harry from the fruit and veg stall in the market had received a rare consignment - bananas. Mother hurried to join the line. While she was waiting, a man went straight to the front and said he had priority because he was a shipyard worker. He was a 'reservist' which meant that because he worked in heavy industry, he did essential war work at home whilst most of the wives in that queue would have had husbands and sons fighting overseas. Many reservists wanted active military service but were obliged to stay. There was however a small number of whom it was said, rightly or wrongly, that they had taken the coward's refuge. So this shipyard shopper with his safe, well-paid 'cushy number' job, felt the full weight of resentment and abuse as he collected his pound of bananas!

It is interesting to reflect that the weekly ration of eggs for Mam and me, was one! So a dozen (not that you could get that many) would have been a three month's supply. We did have dried egg powder which came in stiff packets sealed with wax. On the front was a picture of an eagle; a symbol of the United States of America, who happened to be the supplier.

Brian Watson Cramlington

Bread queues, reminiscent of wartime, stretched along the Borough's streets during the week-long bakers' strike. [*December 1974*]

Delayed deliveries, 1954

Post-War

I'm sure everyone over the age of fifty remembers their 'divi' number. Ours was: 5819. Every time we shopped at the Co-op the assistant would write down how much we had spent and enter our number in a book. We would be handed the small perforated receipt and a carbon copy of the amount went into a book. At certain times of the year there would be queues outside the co-op with wives collecting their accumulated cash bonuses. It was like saving up for something and there was always extra treats on Divi Day.

At our local Co-op there was a female assistant who fascinated me. She had 'cupid lips' that were constantly pursed, ready for kissing I supposed. The male assistant had dark wavy hair that reminded me of the ripples in the Ridley Park lake when I threw a stone in. At the Maypole Dairy there was a sandy-haired chap who would cut slabs of butter from a huge block with a long black knife. He would weigh it and then, with pair of grooved wooden spatulas, he would shape it into a decorative brick, before wrapping it in neatly in greaseproof paper. It seems shopping was a leisurely social occasion when I was younger and you usually came away (after handing over your note) with the purchases in a neatly packed brown paper parcel tied up with string. If one of the items on the list were unavailable, the assistant would write a note on the back for your mam.

What goes into those dozen or so hypermarket plastic bags for today's weekly 'shop'?

Brian Watson Cramlington

Mr Chris Henderson, a Blyth Cooperative Society milk roundsman, was awarded the RSPCA 1952 Horse Merit medal. [*July 1953*]
Four years ago Blyth Cooperative Society owned 39 dray horses and 36 motorised vehicles. Now the society has a fleet of 99 motors and only 5 horses. [*October 1957*]

The last Blyth Co-op horse is put to pasture. [*January 1959*]

GHOSTS OF REGENT STREET, BLYTH

Once a high stone railway bridge
Straddled the road
Beside a busy station,
Full of life.

A rosy-cheeked woman,
Dressed in black
Sat outside with her creel.

Along Regent Street,
Half-built ships were seen
Men creating new life
In the heart of the town.

A buzzer sounded.
From the shipyard gates
Came a wave of bicycles
Four abreast.

Regent Street, Blyth

Under the bridge,
First of a row,
Turnbull's 'baccy' shop;
Well-polished counter
And gleaming brass scales
Gave light to the darkness inside,
With its lingering smell
Of tobacco and snuff.

Where did they go?

Now the fine Keel Row precinct
And expanded market-place.
A Sport's Centre and Civic Centre,
New reasons for pride.

But among the ghosts
Local people remain,
Down-to-earth
Feet-on-the-ground
Friendly.

As they have always been.

Dorothy Redpath Blyth

Floods marooned shoppers and water poured into Regent Street houses in Blyth's worst storm this year. [*January 1954*]

Practical Maths.
Children of East Hartford visit
Brockwell Shopping Centre
Cramlington

THE MUSIC GOES ROUND AND ROUND...

Rock At The Roxy

The Roxy in the early 1960's was still hanging on as a dance hall and there were rock 'n' roll nights. I remember there was a regional competition for local groups and the star performers were the Sixteen Strings, a group from Whitley Bay. At that time everybody wanted to be Cliff Richard and the Shadows. The Blyth audience were tolerant when the Sixteen Strings did their Shadows-type dance routine; they were quite good and living up to their 'semi-professional' billing, but it was downhill when the singer came on. The vocalist was a blonde lad who looked like small version of Billy Fury and he

didn't half fancy himself. His voice was OK but his big mistake was turning up at the Roxy in a blue lurex suit. When he sang the ballad 'Lonely Blue Boy' dead dramatic, on his knees, he took some stick from the lads.. and the lasses weren't too impressed either. This was Blyth not Las Vegas!

It was round about this time that a new record shop was opened in Blyth. It was where Burtons is now. I remember Gary Walker of the Walker Brothers came to open it and there were near-riots. Loads of police were called in to keep the crowds back. His hit at the time was 'Make it Easy on Yourself'! There must be something about the townsfolk that makes them turn out by the thousand to see celebrities. My mam reckoned when the 1950's crooner Dickie Valentine came to Blyth they had to close Waterloo Road because the crowds were in danger of being knocked down. And I wonder how many people remember Kevin Keegan coming to open Prestos (now Safeways). He was an England and Liverpool player at the time and had no connection with Newcastle United. I wasn't there but I heard that it was total mayhem. Once again police protection was called for and I have seen a photograph of the opening ceremony which shows a terrified Kevin Keegan fighting his way through a police cordon. In the 1970's he had the status of a pop star and obviously the same popularity!

Susan Newsham

> Local parents of be-bopping teenagers were concerned that their children were travelling 36 miles to Anfield Plain at week-ends and returning home in the early hours. [*April 1956*]

Dance Band Days

In the 1930's and early 1940's Sunday was a day of rest away from work. The shops and cinemas were closed and the noisy industrial clamour and clangour were replaced by a more harmonious sound - music! The Salvation Army band played on street corners and the Boy's Brigade marched to the Zion Church in Waterloo Road whilst the Wellesley School Bugle Band rent the air as they marched the half-mile to St Cuthbert's Church.

For most young people Sunday afternoon was a walk along the 'prom' and a chance to meet with the opposite sex but for others it was the Bandroom in Edward Street or the Miners' Welfare (now the Civic Centre) where they had the opportunity to learn to play trumpet or trombone or euphonium or even the big bass drum. And what training ground this proved to be. Many a youngster moved on to play with local dance bands whilst others with more ambition and talent went on to be professional musicians.

From an early age I watched my father playing trombone with the LNER Brass Band and longed to join in with them. But I had been taught to play the piano and by the time I was fifteen, I had my own group of players - Johnny Stenhouse and His Band. Before, during, and after the Second World War, there was a demand for live dance music. There was a naval base in the town and there were army bases in the area and entertainment was sorely needed. We began our playing days in St Wilfrid's Hall in Lynn Street, playing for the 'tanner' dance on Fridays and Saturdays. Most nights in the week there would be a dance held somewhere and each little hall had its band and band leader. Raymond Hall had a 'big' band at the Assembly Rooms at Ballast Hill, Steve Hogg was leader at the Bandroom and the New Delaval Pavilion, known to locals as the 'piv'. Tommy Bell was in the Tudor's (later named the Roxy) whilst Peter Cosimini, Kevin McLaughlin, George and Billy Mason, Billy Hall, Austin Conneally and Danny Haggerty all ran successful local bands.

Dances apart, there were wedding receptions to play for and there were also church 'Socials' which were more of a family affair with cups of tea and a chat finishing up with a dance or two. To build up a library of music the leader would join a Music Club run by the (then) music publishers. For an annual fee of twenty-five shillings - a goodly sum in those days - you would be sent four band arrangements per month. These would be a mixed lot; a waltz maybe or a quickstep or some of the more popular tunes of the day. So by joining a few clubs the leader would soon build up a wide ranging assortment of music. Any special items e.g. the Lancers or Eightsome Reels or Dashing White Sergeant or copies for specialist formation dancing could be obtained from the 'Brons' who were also suppliers of music stands and instrument stands and other dance band accessories. The owner, Mr Bron was actually the father of Eleanor Bron the famous actress.

For most young people the event of the week was the Roxy and Tommy Bell and His Band. Many a marriage had its beginnings in a meeting in the Roxy and many a serviceman had happy memories of his nights spent dancing there. Like all big dance halls of the era, the Roxy was known far and wide and became synonymous with enjoyment. There were also the Big Dances, the special social occasions; like the Quaysiders or the Shipyard Dance or the Policemen's Ball and perhaps the biggest of them all, the Mayor's Ball. These would often attract big (professional) bands and I well remember Johnny Dankworth playing at the Roxy with Cleo Laine and a young Dudley Moore on Piano.

Tickets for these affairs were hard to come by and even though they were formal occasions and preceded by the obligatory Whist Drive, they were the highlights of the social calender with tickets as high as 5/-.

Bands had to be very flexible and very versatile. The usual dance programme might include fifteen or twenty dances ranging from a Quickstep and Slow Fox-trot to a Moonlight Saunter to a Half Waltz Cotillion - hence the need for a large library! As the front man, I had to be receptive to the needs of the dancers; I was always thinking ahead to keep the musical momentum and the entertainment going.. it was a balancing act and not easy to gauge. There were nights when everything fell into place. On those occasions the pleasure from the floor was tangible, and if our playing was good, then it was immensely satisfying.

Sunday lunchtime at the Prince of Wales on Waterloo Road was where the bandsmen would meet and exchange stories on the previous night's gig. If a bandleader needed a drummer or clarinetist to sit in for the following week they would always find someone to make the number up. Most of the players had day jobs of course. They worked in the shipyard or in offices of the building trade but once they left their overalls behind and donned their band uniforms, they were 'entertainers' and felt like professionals, even though they were only being paid the Musicians' Union rate of five shillings an hour!

Some of the most memorable gigs took place over holiday week-ends. A Saturday dance had to finish before the stroke of midnight - the never-on-Sunday rule was very strict - however organisers still managed to meet the huge popular demand by holding Monday dances in the early hours. At one minute past twelve in the New Hartley Memorial Hall on Easter Monday, Whit Monday and August Bank Holiday, Johnny Stenhouse and his Band, would be poised and ready to play non-stop until 5 am. Hundreds flocked across the fields from Blyth in the pitch black, to return home as dawn was breaking. There was never a hint of trouble. We had our own transport which was the first milk train of the morning from Hartley Station, delivering us and our instruments, back to Blyth. We had some wonderful nights; the dances ran for years.

Towards the end of the 1950's the bands began to move out of the small church halls and into hotels as Dinner Dances gained in popularity. This period coincided with that other musical phenomena: Rock 'n' Roll. Another generation with its own brand of music emerged and with it came disc jockeys and sound systems that made live dance music redundant. The Working Men's Clubs built concert rooms onto their premises and began booking the emerging rock bands and pop groups and the dance band as such became a bit 'old hat' so far as the younger generation were concerned and the dance band era slowly came to an end. The music of the Big Bands still lives on however and people still like to hear Glenn Miller tunes, evoking as it does, many happy memories.

For all my musician friends, many of them sadly no longer with us, our time is past and a new music has taken its place where dancing with your arms around your partner is no longer appropriate. Our music was of its time and I was pleased to be a part of it. If I have a regret, it is that so many of those large venues have gone. I have always felt that the coming together of people to enjoy a communal experience has a strong unifying effect on the town. It generates a sense of belonging and a sense of pride. It is a great pity that there are few places where crowds can meet. It is a loss to the town and to the young people who may never experience community gatherings.

John Stenhouse Blyth

A Young Band Leader 1947

Blyth holds its first rock 'n' roll competition at the Roxy Ballroom [*January 1957*]

Festival

The 1995 Blyth Festival was a good time. Many local bands gathered to play on the dunes of Links Road on the way to Seaton Sluice. It took a bit of organising but everyone chipped in and made it a great success. The best of Blyth's groups played under a large covered-in tent and people flocked towards it with their six-packs. They sat on the sand and really enjoyed this free live concert. There were complaints beforehand that we might be too noisy or that there would be litter.. or other 'things' going on. We were miles from any housing estates and there was never going to be any bother, we were just there for the music and to be with our friends. As it got darker more people arrived and settled themselves down. The weather was mild, which helped. There was a police presence but the only disturbance was in the car park when a lad had a row with his girlfriend; he wanted to stay but she had to go home. It was a great feeling being with two hundred like-minded friends listening to our music in the open air. It wasn't exactly Woodstock, but I'm sure we all felt something of that shared spirit.

Andy Treadwell BRIC, Blyth

800 young people attend the Big Beat Ball organised by Blyth Cricket Club. [*Sep. 1971*]

OASIS

[Oasis concert, Whitley Bay Ice Rink. January 1996]

Life is a desert...

Friday
Middle of January
With school coming a poor second
And a bus that left at four,
We took our leave and left,
Early.

A cold wait
For a door to open
And a band to play
The songs in our heads
Of longing
And living
Our lives, our way.

Glaring lights and solid sound
Vitality and rhythm,
Escape.
A feeling that cannot be lost,
Cannot be taken,
Mislaid,
Or faked.

Steven Holland
Sixth Form, Blyth Ridley

Music at the Keel Row 1992. Blyth Kingsway First School sing carols for the Christmas Shoppers

Sting, leader of the rock band 'Police' talks on national radio about his teaching experiences at St Peter's Middle School, Cramlington. [*September 1980*]

Our Parties

There's about seventeen of us altogether, a mix of male and females. We've been friends for a few years but many of us have known certain members of the group since we were very little. Not only are most of us in Ridley High's Sixth Form but we see each other at weekends and some evenings too; either going out or meeting in each others homes.

But the weekends to remember are those when a house is left empty by gallivanting parents, who have naively left their offspring alone with instructions to "act sensibly" and not to "do anything stupid." These weekends are few and far between so when they eventually happen they have to be taken advantage of.

The evening celebrations can start.. well, whenever we want, we have a free house to use haven't we? The girls arrive after the lads, mainly because all the girls live in a different area of Blyth and secondly because it takes us longer to get ready. We get there to find the lads have already taken root with their supply of cans around them. On the table is a small offering for us; our beverages.

The music is already playing and laughter is coming from a room where everyone is sprawled over the furniture or the floor. In one of the bedrooms a pile of sleeping bags, pillows, quilts, extra supplies and other baggage accumulates.

Soon the small gathering gets louder and livelier. The volume of the music increases and so does the laughter and talking. Everyone is totally relaxed with their friends and with their environment. After all, we're in charge, no-one can come in and spoil the atmosphere or break up the happy party. After a while the party fragments into smaller groups who want to do different things; the ones who want to talk etc. sit on the stairs or on an upstairs landing. Minglers go and chat in the kitchen and the dancers have control of the music - Offspring, Blur, Oasis, Alanis Morrisette - whatever the mood is, or whatever energy-levels are left.

The dancing-mingling-talking-partying goes on until everyone is too tired to do anything else but sleep. It is then that the mountains of bedding are raided and flattened and everyone finds the most comfortable spot to try and get some rest.

After a few hours the sun comes up and we are awoken by the sound of the early risers who need to be out and away. Sleep-filled eyes try to focus on the mystery person lying beside them who had kept elbowing them through the four hours of sleep they were trying to get. The once neat piles of CD's, brought in the night before, are everywhere, scattered in unbelievable places. There is a stirring, and zombies begin to traipse around the house with soggy eyes and mist-filled heads.

Cups of strong tea and strong coffee are prescribed, then the cleaning up begins. Everyone chips in and it doesn't take too long. Sleeping bags are packed away, coats put on and apologies for making fools of ourselves are sheepishly made. Half of the party make their way out and through all the upheaval a voice is heard from the door:

"Right, 7 o'clock tonight then.. again?"

"Yeah."

A chorus of weak, but perking-up voices, call back.

Sarah McMillan

Sixth Form, Blyth Ridley High School

Dance in Aid of Delaval Football Team – 1954. In The Rex, Whitley Bay   Tom Allan Collection

Owen Brannigan, the Annitsford singer, took part in a charity concert at the Presbyterian Church, Blyth. [*March 1955*]

Anne Guthrie and Kathleen Wilder, former Blyth girls and stars of Covent Garden Royal Opera House, gave a celebrity concert in aid of the United Reform Church restoration fund. £100,000 is needed to repair the town's tallest building. [*March 1985*]

Centre 64

Friday night was the big night of the week. That was when we went to Centre 64. At 14 years of age, the Disco at Centre 64 with Sharon, Julie, Pauline and Lorraine was the most important event in our lives. We'd prepare for it by meeting in each others homes and practicing dance routines in bedrooms. Top of the Pops was our inspiration. We memorised every new dance step. Dancing Queen by Abba was one of the big hits and we worked out a dance to that and couldn't wait to try it out. The great thing about Centre 64 was that you knew everybody and the DJ would play what you asked for. So we requested Dancing Queen and the five of us made a line and danced our dance. It was brilliant.

We got our make-up from Woolworth's. We wore Mary Quant eye crayons; a slash of white with a sky-blue liner. Nobody bothered with lipstick but we always had a Rimmel spot-stick handy. We used this to cover up our acne. It was the colour of sun tan and we dabbed it on, but if anything, it highlighted the spots.

Chewing gum was part of the image too. Bazooka Joe was best because you could pull it out of your mouth in a long stretch then twirl it round your finger.. it seemed cool at the time!

Saturday was a good too. We spent what little money we had on records; it was 50p for a '45' single. We bought our records from the Music Box in Bowes Street then we would pile into the Tudor Cafe next door. We spent hours chattering over a cup of coffee. The cafe with its ceiling beams, horse brasses and pictures of hunting scenes was a regular haunt and they didn't seem to mind that we didn't spend much.

If you wanted to know what was going on in the world then you had to buy your copy of 'Jackie' and 'Smash Hits' from the newsagents. Sharon and I were big fans of the group Kenny and we loved dancing to their song 'The Bump' but then we read that the record was made by session musicians and we felt cheated. I remember cutting up their vinyl disc with a pair of scissors.

Our great loves though, were the Bay City Rollers. Each of us had our own personal roller. I cut my hair and dressed like Les McEwen, the lead singer; people even said I looked like him. I had all the tartan panels in my jacket and baggy pants and I screamed with the rest of the fans when they came to the City Hall in Newcastle. The place was heaving and I came home with only one platform shoe.

My dad wasn't impressed with my appearance. If he saw me coming in Blyth he'd say to my mam, 'Let's cross the road!"

There was always records played in our house, I grew up with music in the background. My mam would play the Beatles songs on a record player that automatically dropped eight singles, one at a time, onto the turntable. Dad liked Elvis, Roy Orbison and Jim Reeves. I often play Beatles songs and it's nice to hear my own children singing along to the tracks.

After the early days at Centre 64 we graduated to the Disco upstairs where there was a different sort of music; not so much pop and the lads were older. Later the Disco at the Golden Eagle pub was a big attraction.

Michelle Gregory Blyth

> Chris Szwagtis, the world champion disco hod dancer, was in Blyth raising funds for kidney sufferers. [*February 1979*]

Quadrophenia

Michelle and I used to go to Blyth Rugby Club and that could be a strange experience. In the summer of 1978 the film Quadrophenia was around and that was quite influential. It glorified the Mods of the 60's, and The Who, with their aggressive style, were back in fashion. The heavy-metal lads and the punks also went to the rugby club and it made for an odd mixture. If the DJ played punk music anyone could get up but the punks let you know that this was their dance and a few elbows could be flying around. Curiously enough 'City Kids' by the Pink Fairies seemed to have a unifying effect and it bridged the wide musical gulf. The rugby club was not a place for the faint-hearted, but the music was good.

Michelle's cousin Paul Lamb inherited a mouth-organ from his grandad and he was always keen on playing blues music. His dad worked at Bate's Pit but Paul was into the music business. He might not be a household name in Blyth but in the United States rock world he is a huge success with his band Paul Lamb and the Kingsnakes. He has played harmonica for Eric Clapton, Dire Straits and many of America's top blues bands.

At local family gatherings the most popular request is "Play the train!". Paul's impressions of British Rail locomotives are legendary in Cowpen Farm Estate.

Martin Gregory Blyth

Four Fingers Club

In the early 1990's myself, Oliver Griffin, and a few friends with an interest in music got together and arranged gigs in Blyth. We started off by inviting local bands to play and we would book a room in a pub. There would be 60 to 100 people coming along so we got a bit more ambitious and spread our net a bit wider. We attracted bands from Glasgow and even Holland but the one that really stands out was the Chumbawamba gig.

Chumbawamba were a punk-style Leeds band with a growing reputation. We reckoned that we could probably sell 100 tickets at £2 a time so we took 50 to a record shop in Newcastle on the off-chance that they would get sold. They were snapped up in two days! So we sent 50 more and they went just as quickly. We were well enough organised but we hadn't anticipated the popularity of the band, and our venue, upstairs at the Steamboat Inn in Blyth was totally inadequate - especially after we had put up the staging, PA's and screens for the group. On the night, over 200 turned up at the door, from as far as London and Wales; the band had quite a following! I still cannot believe we packed them into that small space. Everyone was shoulder to shoulder; you couldn't move. The beer sales were actually down because no-one could get near the bar.

The band were brilliant although it was really scary when they started their set. The Chumbawambas are an exciting group and their fans came to dance. I was trapped in the middle of the room when the music began and people around me started jumping to the beat. I swear the floorboards dropped a good six inches and it wasn't my imagination because three songs later one of the bouncers from the door downstairs came charging up and burst through the crowds yelling for the music to stop.

We had been anxious upstairs, but below, they were terrified! They thought the ceiling was going to come down on top of them. The band stopped and we had to explain the situation. Michelle got onto the stage and took the mike and said that unless everyone sat down for the rest of the set then the gig would have to be called off. Everyone co-operated and in spite of creating even more of a crush on the floor there was still plenty of dancing done - with arms and upper body. It was such a successful evening and you could honestly say that Chumbawamba nearly brought the house down!

We shared out the proceeds with the band and they would only take £150; at the time their fee was about £400. The support bands had a bonus that night. We continued to have some excellent gigs and even Radio Five paid us a visit and featured The Four Fingers Club in an early outside broadcast programme.

Martin Gregory Blyth.

Five Live 1991

It was a strange experience hearing the Radio Five programme. When the recording team were up here looking at the music scene, I sang one of my songs 'The Weather in Blyth', but no-one had any idea when, or even if, it would go out on air. A week or so later I was getting a lift back home from Wallsend when I remembered the broadcast. We were driving along the coast just past Gloucester Lodge and I wondered if the programme had gone out. I fiddled about with the car radio - I had no idea where the channel was on the dial. Then suddenly and mysteriously I found it.. exactly at the start of my song, right on the opening bars.. it was weird! Telepathic?

The weather in Blyth is changing
Sometimes it's hot
Other times it's not
But it's always weather
Weather from the sun and the sky
The weather in Blyth

Sometimes it can be foggy
And wind can blow
And rain can flow
But it will change
That's the weather in Blyth

It may even be wet
When your hoping for a tan
It rarely listens
To the weatherman

It may rain in June
And it very often does
And then you'll be forced to stay inside
And you'll blame it on the weather
The weather in Blyth

Puddles may lie by the roadside
But the people still haven't learned
To be concerned
About more important things than weather
It's raining outside there now
The weather in Blyth

Barnaby Griffin Blyth

Blyth's Theatre Royal echoed to the sound of over fifty German voices following a visit from the Solingen Male Voice Choir. [*June 1963*]

Blyth Amateur Operatic Society give two performances of 'Desert Song' in Solingen, Germany. [*June 1965*]

Dad [Extract]

Tommy Bell at The Roxy 1950

The new Roxy Ballroom was opened in the town and a Learner's Night was held every Thursday. My friends and I thought it would be nice to learn ballroom dancing and as it finished earlier than the usual dances I felt sure I would be able to go. What a laugh! Even when I went to parties at the church I had to come home about an hour before everyone else. So, yes I could go to the Roxy, but I had to leave early! I only went twice to the Learner's Night. It was so humiliating having to leave my friends to come home alone. I shed tears of frustration as I walked back. It became a standing joke among my friends when we tried to make arrangements. "Dorothy will have to ask her dad" they would say. It was not meant unkindly but it hurt. I can still remember the feeling as if it were yesterday. That kind of stifling does nothing for morale, or for your social life.

Dorothy Redpath Blyth

> A 17 stone Manchester housewife broke her own non-stop piano playing record by sixty minutes, in a 133 hour musical marathon which packed Blyth's Theatre Royal for a week. 21,000 people saw her play; a record for any one show since the theatre was built. [*August 1958*]

Evening In Paris?

When I was a teenager in the mid-60's I used to like listening to the hit parade and often the tunes would be ringing around in my head throughout the day. On one occasion my dad sent me to Barrons the Chemist to get some perfume for my mam's birthday. I told them what I wanted and they looked puzzled. I explained that my mam always wore it and it came in a small navy blue bottle with a tiny rubber stopper on the inside. I was dead embarrassed by this time. They said "Oh you mean Evening in Paris?" I said, no, that wasn't it. After a while they convinced me and I took it home. I was sure my dad was going to send me back but he just said "Aye, that's the one."

Later on I was listening to the radio and I heard Kenny Ball and his Jazzmen playing their latest hit 'Midnight in Moscow'. That was it, that's what I'd asked for at the chemist, 'Midnight in Moscow'. It must have stuck in my subconscious. I was close but it was the wrong time and the wrong place wasn't it?

Mick Davison Blyth

Mr John Gair Robson composer of 'Where ivvor you gan yor sure to find a Geordie' died at his home age 71. [*January 1957*]

Tommy Swanson, now aged ninety, continues to play the organ at St Paul's Church, Seaton Sluice, as he has done for 56 years. [*January 1985*]

Brass Band

We had just moved into our Victorian house at the top of Waterloo Road in Blyth and we spent the first night in an attic bedroom. At 8 o'clock the following morning we were woken by the sound of distant music. We pulled back the curtains and watched the approach and departure of the Cowpen and Crofton Colliery Brass Band as they marched past on their way to the bus station, and as I later learned, the Miners' Picnic at Atlee Park, Bedlington. It was a magnificent sight.. and sound. The proud banner was held high, the uniforms were immaculate, and the early sun flashed and dazzled on the gleaming brass instruments. Those few minutes set me up for the day as I cheerfully emptied boxes and started on the decorating.

Twelve hours later, we heard it again.. the same swelling brass band sound. We rushed to the front door and sure enough, they were back; retracing their steps to the Miners' Welfare.. although the steps were not quite so steady. The banner was still held high, and if several of the bandsmen's uniforms looked a little disheveled, their music was still superb. The leader walked with his head high and not without cause, for tucked under his arm was the winner's cup. I imagine it had held several pints of beer.. briefly!

It was a wonderful introduction to the town. Had they arranged this uplifting 'march past' for our family's benefit? It certainly seemed that way at the time.

Bill Blyth

> Cowpen and Crofton Workingmen's Band, North East area winners, took second place in the National Coal Board Brass Band Championships held at Blackpool. [*October 1962*]

Backworth Brass Band at Blyth Market Place. June 1996

I WAS A MINER...

A Coal Career

I left St Wilfrid's School in Blyth at the age of fifteen without any qualifications and had a choice of three jobs. Shop delivery boy, shipyard worker or miner. Coal mining was the best paid so it was an easy decision to make. There were plenty of collieries at the time and I believe Crofton, Isabella and Cambois were still working in the mid '60's. I chose Bates Pit and after three months training at Astley School in Seaton Sluice I worked on the surface until I was sixteen.

Sixteen was the age when apprenticeships began in most trades and for the next five years the lads would 'serve their time'. In the pit you made progress by working hard and proving your worth. At sixteen you went underground; 1,000 feet below. There was about a hundred on each shift and the cage carried 36 men, 18 on top 18 underneath. You had been well-trained in advance and you knew what to expect. My first job was to supply the face workers with their wooden props. We used the ponies to pull in the timber. The props had to support the roof of the area that had been worked out. The part of the seam that was being worked might be 200 yards long [200m] and three foot [1m] deep. You started cutting at the far end and worked back over, propping as you went. The timbers were always creaking and you could see them bending under the weight from above. The first break was always the worst; this was when the roof would suddenly drop. There would be a loud groan and a whoop then forty yards or so of displaced air would be forced out towards you down the narrow walkways at quite a force. When the break came everyone ran for it. It could be really scary. Even the older miners never quite got used to the sudden fall of rock - you could see the fear in their faces.

The lads worked with the ponies before they were face-trained. I was given a pony named Lawyer and I think he came from the New Forest area. There were two stables down below and they housed about twenty horses each. The walkways were fairly wide at Bates so the ponies were bigger than the smaller galloways found at other pits. All ponies were male; stallions and geldings - there were no mares - and there was some bad 'uns amongst them. It was their aggressive natures that made them suitable for the work load. Lawyer though, was a lovely beast. It had a lot to do with how you treated them; they worked better on kindness My mother used to give me two baits, one for me and one for Lawyer, his was often the biggest! There was nothing that horse couldn't pull. Lawyer worked the same shift as me, year in and year out; he became more like a pet. He would be waiting when I arrived and at the finish of his stint he was happy to be hosed down and returned to his dry stable. When I moved on Lawyer was taken over by my mate, who was also very attached to him. It wasn't such a wrench leaving him behind because I knew I'd left him in good hands. I don't know how I would have reacted if he'd been given a rough owner.

As a child I can remember seeing all forty of the ponies from Bates Pit being led to a field where Malvin's Close School is now. They always let them out for the miners' annual two-week summer holiday and as soon as their hooves touched the grass they would go mad. These cooped-up ponies would leap and jump about in their new-found freedom. It must have been quite a holiday for the ponies too because the kids would come and feed them every day. By the time I worked at

Isabella Colliery 1950

74

Bates they had stopped bringing them to the surface. Apparently it was such a job to get them back down the pit again that the managers decided it wasn't worth the effort. Lawyer was twelve years old when he worked for me but by the time most ponies reached twenty, they had served their usefulness and were put out to grass or sold to local traders.

It is no secret to say that money was the motivation for the miners. If you grafted you were paid well. It was the ambition of most of the young lads to get on a team of like-minded piece workers. In the mid-60's you still had to wait your turn and hope that one of the men would leave so you could

> For the first time in the history of the local mines, the ponies at Isabella, Bates and the Mill pits, stayed underground during the miners' annual fortnight holidays. [*July 1961*]

step into their place. For six months to a year, the newly-trained lads were on 'spare' until a permanent opportunity arose. During this time you got to know the job and the men by working in all parts of the pit. My time finally came and I worked with a good team. It was hard physical work but I enjoyed it. For young men with boundless energy and strength it was a great test and challenge to their manhood. Strong bonds developed amongst the men and teams. There was the shared satisfaction of a tough shift and also the knowledge that your efforts had filled your mate's pay packet as well as your own.

When I was twenty-one I saw my first fatality. By then I was face-trained and keen to get fixed up with a team of men. I was doing a temporary shift when the word came round that there had been a fall of stone and two men were hurt and another had died. Everyone of course, stopped work for the day. It was out of respect for their colleague but it also affected every miner deeply as it was a reminder of the dangers of this high-risk job. I was working nearby and asked to help. When I arrived the injured men were being treated for minor injuries, I think one had a fracture, but what struck me forcibly was the dead man. His body had been placed to one side and although he had a wound on his head it was difficult to accept that his injuries were fatal and final. There was nothing more that could be done for him so all the activity was centred around the living. I helped carry out the stretcher and it took a long time to get over the incident. At twenty-one you only think about living for the moment but down there I was faced with an unexpected death and I felt vulnerable for the first time in my life.

After a few years as a face-worker I was accepted onto a course to train as a deputy. I was told there might be resentment from the men but I never found any at Bates. The deputy carries a tremendous responsibility. He has to make sure the place of work is safe and ready for the men to start their shift. There is a saying: 'All accidents are preventable' and if anything went wrong underground the deputy was accountable. I never had a fatality in the years I was a deputy but it was a real fear that hung over the job. Money drove the men on and some miners would be reckless and take risks if you didn't watch them. I know some men thought that deputies were petty and officious, but you had to insist that they 'supported' their work as they went. Of course, fitting the props meant leaving the coal to spend valuable earning time on a non-productive task. They would get so absorbed they lost sight of the safety and had to be reminded quite forcibly at times.

There were some incredible workers and one team of three young lads I had to oversee would get their heads down and graft non-stop. Of course they neglected the supports and I had to tell them. They protested so I turned off their power. "You might make a million pounds.." I told them "..but you cannot spend it if you're dead!" I got through to them eventually.

Michael Thompson Cyprus

'The greatest day since the signing of the Magna Charter..' The NCB takes coal mines into state ownership. [*January 1947*]
The 150 year old Seghill Colliery, which had once employed 1200 men, closed down. [*October 1962*]

New pithead baths were opened at Bates Pit [*April 1951*]

Crofton Mill

At Crofton Mill pit, before the days of the pithead baths in the 1950's, miners would emerge through the gates of the colliery and wait at the bus stop opposite; black with coal dust. They were still in their working gear and they waited for the bus on their hunkers, smelling musty and dank. Behind them the very large advertising hoardings showed Zoe Newton, the milk girl with the fringe hairstyle. A smaller red print poster told the public who Newcastle United's latest opponents would be at St James' Park and a black and white bill alongside advertised boxing and wrestling at the New St James' Hall.

Brian Watson Cramlington.

Shock news of the year; twelve Northumberland pits are to close in the next two years. The future of another eight is doubtful. [*November 1965*]

One of Northumberland's oldest pits, the Isabella Colliery, shut down after 115 years of production. [*February 1966*]

Kramel Kid [extract]

When we moved up the road to High Pit in a Coal Company tenancy where there was no electricity, only gas, but it did have two gardens. My dad had his bath in front of the fire every time he came home from the pit and we all had to go away and come back later. My brother and I were given 'pay pennies' for our pocket money every payday but on October 19th 1928 Father came upstairs to wake us up. He needed our pennies because Mother wasn't well and he wanted the money to put in the gas meter to keep the light on. Next morning, surprise surprise! There was a lovely baby sister. It was the first we knew of it.

Leslie Miners Cramlington

Bates Pit, the 'push-button' showpiece colliery of East Northumberland entered the 500,000 ton-of-coal-a-year field with the completion of its new 1000 foot shaft [300 metre] [*January 1961*]

The NCB announced that a series of revolutionary new powered roof supports costing £1.5m were to be installed at Bates Colliery [*December 1982*]

Our Visit To Bates Colliery

[Crofton Junior School project 11-11-71]

Miners at Bates Pit, Holywell

Tom Allan Collection

Yesterday Mrs Reid took a group of children to Bates Colliery. When we first went in we saw a carving of a pitman's head. We thought it was made of brass or metal, but when we got closer, we realised it was made of wood because we could see the grain. The wood was from the pit. There was a lamp on the man's helmet.

Then we went into a room where there was a man sitting. There were lights on his desk. He told us about them. There were six telephones on his desk and if one rang a light would flash.

After that we went into a very noisy room and there was a big wheel with a rope going round. This was the winding room.

Then we went outside and went up a lot of stairs. We came to a room where the coal was. The coal was being put into trucks. Then the trucks went under a steel shed and all the coal was tipped out.

Everything was done by machinery. We saw television screens which showed what was going on all over the colliery. Then we went under a long tunnel and there was a conveyor belt with coal on it. As the coal was going along it was being weighed. When we got to the top of the tunnel there were two giant magnets like hands. We were throwing metal onto it and it stuck. Mr Dunn threw a bit of metal on the belt and it jumped off the coal and onto the magnet.

We went to see the coal getting washed. The man was using something like a hose.

Afterwards we went outside and saw a lovely view and some cranes like giraffes. Mrs Reid took some photographs. After that we went on a barge which carries the waste materials out to sea. We saw the engines of the barge and when we looked at the river there were two lovely swans.

Yvonne Tochaile (age 11)

General Strike

A memorial service was held for the 204 men and boys who died 100 years ago in Northumberland's worst pit disaster at New Hartley [*January 1962*]

Behind the brick factory at East Cramlington was a filthy pool where the coals were washed It was silted up with waste products. During the 1926 strike many youngsters took their bogies and prams to the pool and filled boxes up with the black silt and brought them home. When they got back they shaped the mud into balls and put them out to dry in the sun. These 'cakes proved to be effective fuel for the fires because there were no free coal deliveries when the strike was on. The owners didn't object either; it helped clear out an unsightly pool.

Arthur Heayns Klondyke

National coal strike begins. Miners demand 'Coal not Dole!' [*March 1984*]
Arthur Scargill promised to 'fight to the bitter end' when speaking to miners at a march and rally held in Blyth. [*May 1984*]

Blyth MP John Ryman vowed to fight 'tooth and nail' to prevent the closure of Bates Pit after an official 'leak' detailed the shut down of the High pit by 1987-88 [*November 1984*]
Miner's strike is over. Men return to Bates Pit. [*March 1985*]

The 1984/5 strike was a very unhappy period. The deputies were obliged to keep the collieries safe and as a result we were not on strike with the men; mind you, not one deputy at Bates crossed the picket line. We felt for the working miners who genuinely believed in 'Coal no Dole'. There was hardship, and I was full of admiration for the ordinary lads who held out to the end. There was bitterness too, which was a great pity as it divided families and communities. Whatever people feel about the dispute there is no denying that the men were fighting for their jobs and events that followed, the shut-down of Bates, proved they had case. When closure was threatened an independent survey revealed that there was still 2 million tons of viable, saleable coal underground. They recommended that the pit stay open for at least another two years. That turned out to be a false dawn; two days later the NCB said it would close, in spite of the evidence.

Michael Thompson Cyprus

Miners at Bates Pit hear the news they have been waiting for: The Independent Colliery Review recommend that the pit be given a two year reprieve. [*February 1986*]

NCB press ahead with closure. NUM concede defeat after High Court ruling that Coal Board's decision could not be challenged. [*March 1986*]

Men at Bates work their last shift as preparations are made to close the pit at the end of the month [*May 1986*].

After Bates

I moved to Ellington but things were changing for the mining community. I was happy to take early retirement. There was so much pressure on the deputies, especially when the NCB started bringing in contractors to do the work. They were an unknown quantity and definitely a mixed bag. A deputy told me it was getting to the stage where he was frightened to go to work.

One Blyth lad went to a private pit (no names) and there was an industrial accident. It was not his fault, but he broke his leg. A couple of days later he turned up on crutches and presented his sick note to the office. They took one look and said "We don't accept these - you're finished." And that was it. The private owners dictate the terms now and that means no union membership. There were many who felt that in the past the NUM were too powerful with their 'closed shop' policies, but there's plenty now who would be glad of the Union's security and protection.

Michael Thompson Cyprus

Speakers at the Northumberland Miners' Picnic, Bedlington:

Mrs Bessie Braddock and Aneurin Bevan [June 1956]
Hugh Gaitskell spoke to a crowd of over 100,000 in the sweltering heat. [1957]
Harold Wilson becomes the first Prime Minister in power to address the Miner's meeting. [1968]
Deputy Labour Leader Michael Foot and Betty Boothroyd MP [1981]

Winding Room [Extract from Kramel Kid]

My father worked as an engineman on the winding engines that raised or lowered the pit cage that carried men and coal out of the depths of the mine. Later he became a 'hauler' and controlled the haulage engine which brought coal up after the men had changed their shift and were safely out of the way. I often had to take extra bait to him if he had been asked to work overtime when his marrer was sick.

In his workplace, I was overawed at the sight of those great flywheels turning and the thick steel rope coiling around the big drum as it reeled the cables in. The unseen part beyond the hole in the wall where it disappeared, mystified me. What was going on out there and down to the bowels of the earth? Coal tubs were being connected to steel ropes, men were pressing buttons which sent bell-ringing signals; so many rings for 'stop' 'go' or 'reverse'. All this in the near darkness which culminated on the wall beside my father's chair. This chair had been joiner-made and was more like a throne. All the while there was the noise of the engines, creaking of timbers, and loud hisses of steam surging out of hot pipes. When nothing was being moved my dad would walk around with an oily rag, wiping the rods, levers and brass equipment. I could have stayed with those mighty wheels and cogs for ever.

Leslie Miners Cramlington

Blyth Harbour coal shipments totalled 162,163 tons for the week ending December 17th; a new record for the port [*December 1960*]

MONDAY IN THE LANE (EXTRACT)

Down the lane past the reek from the middens
Past the door with no sneck, painted brown
Past the leaf-clogged sink and the clothesline hooks
To the street lamp with its remnant of rope
And the wickets chalked white in the grooves
Through the smell of soapy-hot water
And the sheets blowing high in the wind.

There's a miner squatting down on his hunkers
Drawing hard on an after-shift cig
Feeling the sting of the wind on his face
As the breeze chills his black vested chest
Savouring the freshness and cool of up top
After hours in the bowels of the earth
Anxiously unsure of his hold upon life
He doubts every moment, though precious.

Knarled hands and pitted face, bear testimony
To the hard unremitting burden of work,
Old before time, yet proud of his squeaky clean
New found freedom.

John Stenhouse
Blyth

Work began at Bates Colliery to improve some of the less-attractive features of the plant as part of a national campaign to brighten our industrial landscape. [*November 1969*]

Remains of Bates Pithead 1995

ow To Make The Fire Up

Get up early (usually the woman of the house).

It will be freezing cold.

Put the kettle on.

Rake out the grate with the poker and put the re-usable cinders in the hearth on a page from the Blyth News.

In your slippers, carry the ash pan out to the bin.

Go out the door backwards to stop the ashes blowing in your face and down the front of your goonie (dressing gown).

It will be raining.

Bring back a bucket of coal which you have had to shovel in yourself, even though the last person to empty the scuttle was supposed to fill it up again.

Don't forget the sticks.

Roll up pages from the Blyth News and make into tight balls.

Carefully place them in the grate and put the sticks on top.

Use firelighters even though your Mam never used them – she always sprinkled sugar on.

Put the cinders on the sticks and carefully position the best bits of coal over the firelighters.

Your fingers will be cold but try to open the box of matches the right way up to avoid spilling them out.

Light the firelighters and wait.

It never starts straight away, so if you are well-off, get the galvanised steel bleezer that looks like a square shield and cover the fire with it.

The other way to get the fire going is to rest the upright poker on the grate and stretch a large sheet of the Blyth News across the fireplace to create a draught.

After a while this will turn black and burst into flames.

When this happens release the paper up the flue and hope the chimney doesn't catch fire.

The fireplace 'tidy' is likely to be a chromium knight in armour and his sword will be the poker.

Unhook the brush and tiny dust pan from the back and sweep up the hearth.

The debris goes onto the coals along with all the other household waste.

By now the fire will be blazing and its warm flickering glow will fill the room.

Next, go into the kitchen to try to scrub the dirt off your hands and make a cup of tea, for a five minute sit down.

Return to the room and find the entire family and the cat huddled up in front of the fire.

They will not move.

When they ask if there's any tea going, or have you seen the Blyth News? Try to be tolerant.

Andy Griffin Blyth

Dad [Extract]

> Mr Alf Robens, Blyth MP, accepted the chairmanship of the National Coal Board at a salary of £10,000 a year. [*June 1960*]

Dad was always occupied and often I was asked to help. One of his jobs was making 'blazers' these were flat sheets of metal with a handle in the centre which covered the fireplace openings and helped to make coal fires burn up more quickly. I enjoyed watching this from a distance rather than being too near. A short piece of rail was used to make the lip at the base of the blazer. This was the part which sat on the bar at the front of the fire grate. My task was to steady the flat piece of metal on the rail till it was hammered into shape. Vibrations shot up my arm and it felt as if my head would burst. The noise was unbearable. I am sure Dad could not have realised how bad it was; he was slightly deaf himself, and no wonder! It surprises me that it did my hearing no harm. At least it taught me that nothing lasts for ever - I did enjoy the quietness afterwards.

Dorothy Redpath Blyth

> Joe Steel, a 42 year old miner ate 30 packets of crisps in 52 minutes beating his own world record of 29 packets in 63 minutes. [*April 1957*]

> A 20 year old miner, Albert Taylor, plunged fully clothed into the icy river near Ritson's jetty to save two boys, Brian and Kenneth Williamson, who were in danger of drowning. [*January 1956*]

Banking [1950]

As older kids, we used to play on the top of 'the heap'. During the war when fuel was in short supply, we would climb over the mountains of colliery waste and often we'd come home with bits of coal for the fire, although they tended to 'spit'. My mother knew how to economise and if we were going to the pictures or visiting relatives, she would cover the fire with coal dust. This 'banking' as it was called, was safe as well as cost-effective and a finely meshed fireguard would trap the spitting coal and stop it jumping out beyond the fender. By the time we got back the room would be nice and warm with the fire burning merrily. There was always a fleecy rug in front of the hearth, usually rectangular or half-moon in design. The fireplace looked naked without them. I liked to sit and stare at the fire on a basket-woven wooden stool until the veins of my legs stood out with the heat. I would gaze into the embers and watch as they change shape by falling and collapsing.

Washing day was a misery because the fully-laden clothes horse had priority round the fire and it blocked out all the warmth.

Brian Watson Cramlington

Industrial Landscape,
November 1965

A plan to clean up the East Cramlington 'Jaws of Hell' coal tip is given the go-ahead by Blyth Valley Council. [*October 1975*]

The Heaps

As a child I was always told to keep away from the coal heaps.

The Isabella Colliery and the Crofton Mill Pit had large heaps that could be very dangerous. Under the surface there were fires burning and there was a constant smell of sulphur. Tramps had been known to die beside the heaps. They would lie there overnight, perhaps for warmth, but the fumes killed them. Children too had to be wary of the smouldering piles as they could step onto loose ashes and fall into the heap. It was still warm and dangerous in places for several years after the pit had closed down.

Jean Reid

Blyth

It was announced that Blyth's new golf course on the New Delaval pit heap site would soon be under way. [*December 1970*]

Bates Pit, the 'push button' showpiece colliery 1960's

ON THE TOWN...

Saturday [c1984]

Most Saturdays we would play outside in the street on our BMX bikes. Mine was blue and white; it was my pride and joy. My friends and I would get two bricks and a piece of wood from my dad's garden shed to build a ramp. We had competitions to see who could jump the furthest. Those daring enough to use three or four bricks always won, but I never plucked up the courage. We were inspired by Evel Knievel.

Now and again my parents would take us to the pictures in Blyth. I remember the first film that I saw, it was 'Basil, the Great Mouse Detective.' I distinctly remember that day, as it was also the first time that I had tasted peanut butter. I vomited all over the floor in the pictures and missed the end of the film. But what I saw of the film had been excellent.

In summer we used to love going to the park. It was always packed; filled with children of my age who couldn't wait to splash about in the paddling pool. I recall feeling really 'hard' when I managed to get from one side of the monkey bars to the other without stopping.

On Saturday mornings my grandad would take me and my brother to the beach. We would play on the sand or on the big concrete boat for about half-an-hour and then for a special treat we would have a glass of pop and an ice-cream at the old Mermaid Cafe.

But my favourite Saturday activity of all was riding on the roundabout in the marketplace at Blyth. There was always a queue but it was well worth the wait. I used to ride in the aeroplane pretending that I was flying, and when I got off I had to sit down for a while to avoid the embarrassment of falling over. We were always amazed at how the old lady could turn the handle on the roundabout as it seemed to be going at 100 mph. The ride cost twenty pence.

On the way home we would stop at the shop for a sherbet dip or a ten pence mix-up. My favourite sweets were the flying saucers with sherbet in the middle and jelly worms coated with sugar. We always feared putting one extra sweet in the bag by mistake as the shop had a sign which said 'Thieves May be Prosecuted'.. but we did sometimes.

Graham Davison

Sixth Form, Blyth Ridley High School

A plan for Blyth Valley's BMX track got under way after a personal appeal to the Mayor from four keen youngsters. [*February 1983*]

The Orbit

I was involved with Cramlington New Town's free newspaper The Orbit. It started out as The Compass and it was really an extended parish magazine of St Nicholas' Church but it grew as the town developed. Initially the local boy scouts made the deliveries but its circulation soon reached 2,000.

I offered my services as a volunteer photographer and I joined the editorial team which met each month to decide on the content. The costs were shared amongst the County Council and the builders of the town. The Courier [Herald and Post] agreed to slot The Orbit each month into their newspaper and this community information newsheet suddenly received an 18,000 copy circulation in Blyth Valley.

Many people believe The Orbit was instrumental in generating a sense of community in Cramlington. At first there was a belief that the new town was soulless but the list of events showed that this developing conurbation was a lively residential area with colourful local personalities. The church played its part in bringing the people together and no-one could have done more than Father Richard Cass who worked tirelessly for the residents regardless of their religious preferences. He was known affectionately as 'Mr Cramlington'.

Keith Thompson Cramlington

East Cramlington Restoration 1996

Northumberland County Council approved a £50m plan for the first new town in Britain to be built by private enterprise: Cramlington New Town.
[*June 1961*]

Walks Between The Wars [Extract from Kramel Kid]

After chapel on a summer evening many families went for walks. From Klondyke there were several favourite excursions:

1] We would sometimes walk towards the sea through the East Cramlington colliery area, then into the fields, over a stile, and across the road at the north end of Seaton Delaval to reach the Astley Arms, now known by its present name: The Keel Row. Behind the inn was a long walk through the fields to Gloucester Lodge Farm which was almost on the shoreline near Blyth.

2] Or we would walk towards station bridge at Cramlington and pass the airship shed on the way to Winny Fields; an open area that was full of yellow flowering gorse bushes. Our stroll could continue to Plessey Woods which was very popular during the blue-bell season. Or perhaps at the station bridge our route would lead either past the aerodrome or up to Arcot Hall.

3] If we walked through the fields to Seghill we could turn right and follow the track of the old wagon way to West Cramlington. This line was used to transport coal to Percy Main many years ago. A left turn brought us to Seaton Delaval and the railway station, Masonic hall and two chapels. Next there was East Cramlington. This was a very busy compact area with colliery rows, a brickworks, locomotive sheds, workshops, coal-washing plant, the Lamb Pit and the railway crossing.

4] At the Astley Arms (Keel Row) we would go along the High Road which gave splendid views of the North Sea and Blyth Harbour. After we reached Stickley Farm we could turn left to Shankhouse or carry on northwards to the 'Three Horse Shoe Inn' (now 'The Shoes'). From there we walked to Horton church or west to Hartford before returning to Cramlington village.

We used to have some fine walks, but one thing was certain, whichever direction we walked in, you would be sure to pass a coal mine. Where I lived it was possible to count 16 chimneys. Of course then there was no new housing to obstruct your view, it was all just grazing land.

For Sunday School trips we would go to Seaton Sluice. We were taken in horse-drawn 'hay bogies' which were only 12 inches [30 cms] from the ground, or we would travel in a long vehicle with seats along the side called a 'brake'. We would play games and have races on the beach, followed by hearty singing. Then there would be free time when we would walk around the 'town'.

Leslie Miners Cramlington

Airship Shed – 1929, Cramlington   Tom Allan Collection

Blyth Council are to provide a riverside walk to Ha'penny Woods and provide a picnic area at Meggie's Burn. [*December 1974*]

Blyth Council are to spend £150,000 to make Seaton Sluice a popular leisure harbour. They will begin by dredging silt from the river bed. [*May 1973*]

Cramlington Village

Cramlington village is an old part of the town. It has many features like St Nicholas's Church and the glaziers which used to be the old chapel. There is also the Blagdon Arms.

The Blagdon is special to me because I have slept there a number of times. It used to be an inn and coaching house. When people wanted to come for a drink they put their horses in what is now the bottle shed. The Blagdon is a listed building so all the features cannot be changed or moved which includes the old range, fireplaces and stables.

Blagdon Arms Cramlington Village Conservation Area 1992

The Blagdon is supposed to have a ghost who is a friendly old woman. Many of the customers have said they have heard or seen this ghost and some of the staff have witnessed strange goings on in the cellar. The ghost is said to live in the cellar at the far end of the pub. Above, is a solicitor's office which still has an old desk and fireplace, and there used to be stairs to get to it. When the pub was extended and re-decorated they knocked down walls and took away the stairs and discovered an old range which had been hidden for years. Did it belong to the ghostly old woman?

Soon I am moving to Milton Keynes but the best memory I will have of the village was on New Years' Eve when hundreds of people gathered in the village square waiting for the 12 o'clock chimes to bring in the new year. When the bells rang everyone was laughing, cheering and hugging one another. It was an experience I shall never forget.

Sarah Whitehead Age 13 Brockwell Middle School

Major the Hon. Edward Delaval Astley and his bride entertained tenants of Delaval Hall at high tea to celebrate the Major's wedding. [*September 1954*]

John Hedley Patterson aged 74, who had worked at Seaton Delaval Hall for over 60 years, received a chiming clock from Lord Hastings as a token of his service. [*Oct. 1959*]

Pubs And Clubs

There were loads of working men's clubs in Blyth 30 years ago and they were always busy. There's obviously been a decline and maybe that's because there's fewer working men. There was always lots of pubs too, I remember reading local historian Jim Scott's list; there was 92 of them! I once spent a mind-numbing evening in the Waterloo Club with a total stranger who described every one of them from memory by mentally travelling up and down the town's streets. It was the night-out from hell but what a pub crawl that might have been.

I was living in Whitley Bay in the mid-1960's when there was a determined backlash against the 'Fed' culture because the breweries started doing bizarre things to the pubs to pull in the punters. In Tynemouth there was the Beachcomber bar inside the Plaza which was done out to resemble a South Sea island with palm trees, Hawaiian music, and best of all, every twenty minutes there was a tropical rainstorm. Lightning would flash, there would be rolling thunder, and rain would splash into a plastic lagoon in the far corner. All this was happening on the North-East coast, practically on the beach. If they wanted a storm why didn't they just open the windows?

It was at this time that The Seahorse opened in Blyth on Plessey Road. That was a weird place. The pub was obviously inspired by the sea because the carpets, curtains and pictures all had a fishy theme. Mind you the big attraction lay under your feet. The floor was clear glass and underneath there was a vast aquarium. Hundreds of fish were swimming below as you drank your beer. It was a real conversation killer. Customers just sat with their glasses mesmerised by this underwater world. Darts and dominoes didn't seem appropriate; it was like supping in a dentist's waiting room. It gave a whole new meaning to the expression 'getting tanked up'.

Bill Blyth

Vaux Breweries are to change the name of Blyth's oldest and best known hotel from 'The Star and Garter' to 'The Steamboat' [*April 1967*]

A 22 year old man, Evan Thomas Jones, set out from Blyth market place on a 300 mile walk to London pushing two crates of beer loaded on a pram - for a £20 wager! [*November 1961*]

A Sense Of Blyth

Looking, but looking at what?
It's empty, bare
Everyone's gone home.

It's weird to think that just a few hours ago
It was full of people looking for bargains
On the market stalls
Or stopping to chat to friends.

Quiet, but for how long?
Silence
Daylight is approaching

The noise was one of happiness and joy
As the children played in the park
And splashed in the pool
While their parents sunbathed on the grass.

Listening, but listening to what?
Wind, waves
The day begins
The water's laughing laps against the sides of boats.
The gentle whirring of the wind farm is comforting
The cool fresh breeze.

Realising, but realising what?
It's continuity
Day after day after day
The market, the park, the harbour
It's here, the people are happy
I am happy
I'm home.

Lee Taylor
Sixth Form, Blyth Ridley High School

Traffic

I came back to Blyth to take my driving test. I was told it was the best place to go to. They were not wrong. I'd had several unsuccessful attempts at North Shields so when I set off from the Blyth test centre by the quayside I was a bit nervous but it was better than I could have hoped for. In 1964, Blyth didn't have any traffic lights - it's true! The only roundabout was the Broadway Circle (mini-roundabouts hadn't been invented) and amazingly, the only hill for miles was at Ballast Hill down by the river and on the day of my test it was congested so the examiner gave it a

Broadway Circle, Blyth

miss. Also I had chosen a day when the market wasn't on and I had asked for 2 o'clock in the afternoon. You could practically pick your time in those days.

I was in Blyth soon after and the car wouldn't start. It was a terrible day and it was the cold and damp that was stopping the engine from turning over. I got out of the car and suddenly it seemed, from nowhere, half a dozen total strangers appeared to give me a push and get me started again. I've never forgotten that. Would it have happened in Whitley Bay?

Bill Blyth

Housewives near Crofton Mill barricaded their homes to keep out the coal dust. [*June 1949*]
Occupants of Horton Road, Bebside, once a residential beauty spot, protest to the NCB about noise and dust from the new Stepping Stones open cast coal site 50 yards from their homes. [*September 1956*]

Three hundred school children got an unexpected holiday when gales deposited clouds of coal dust on New Delaval. [*June 1962*]

Details were announced of a £3.25m East Northumberland spine road. It will be a 10 mile dual carriageway from Killingworth to Bedlington. [*February 1966*]

Sharp Practice

One day I was at my friend John Bell's house in Cowpen playing darts. We had to be very quiet because his dad was on night shift and he was upstairs asleep. We had the dartboard on the back of the door and John was firing them when his younger brother Steven got in the way. It was horrible, the dart hit him smack on the side of the head by his temple and it stuck in. The funny thing was it didn't seem to hurt him. He got a shock naturally, who wouldn't? He only started bawling when we tried to get it out. We laid him down on the floor and sat on top of him and tried pulling it but we hadn't the strength to shift it. It was stuck, embedded in the bone.

With all the commotion John's dad came downstairs in a terrible temper but he stopped yelling when he saw the dart. I remember he tried removing it but couldn't shift it either, and he was a miner! There was only one thing for it, the hospital.

Mr Bell quickly threw some clothes on and put a woolly hat on Steven. It didn't cover the dart; that still stuck out of the side of his head. It looked funny but nobody was laughing. The four of us waited at the bus stop looking pretty conspicuous. The people at the bus stop were asking "Is that a dart in that laddie's head?" I thought at the time it was a bit of an obvious question. Mr Bell was getting more uncomfortable as he paid for his "one and three halves" because the passengers were showing concern and making enquiries. The buses were always full then and on this day it was no exception. The whole of the upper and lower deck seemed to be discussing the dart in Steven's head and they all had an opinion about it.

We were glad to get off the bus and over the road into the Thomas Knight hospital. They saw Steven straight away and I don't know what the doctors did exactly but in less than ten minutes we were back outside waiting to catch a bus again, with the dart in Mr Bell's pocket. There had been no blood, no scars, nothing to show for the ordeal.. quite disappointing really.

Mr Bell didn't say much about the whole business but when we got home but he took the dartboard off the door, pocketed the other two darts, then went back to bed.

Mick Davison

Blyth

Bus Station, Blyth

Blyth residents were told that beetles in drinking water was no cause for concern. [*August 1951*]

Housewives at Isabella Colliery are seeking the installation of electricity in an effort to bring the housing 'up-to-date' [*March 1955*]

Snowdrift

For twenty-five years at Seaton Delaval Colliery I had lived within walking distance of the Time Office and colliery yard but when I transferred to Bates Pit in Blyth, travelling was clearly the big difference. It was a distance of 7 miles. At Bates Pit I worked shifts, so public transport, especially at week-ends, was out of the question. But I had two faithful friends in my hut at home - namely bicycles! Having been a keen cyclist from the age of 15 years, cycling as a hobby was all I thought about; almost every day (definitely every Sunday) all the year round. I was now 42 years old (1960) and cycling to Bates Pit was not going to be a problem.

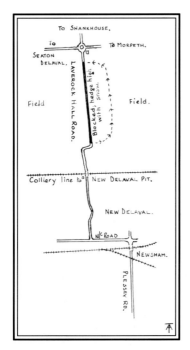

The bike I used to ride was a lightweight BSA Tour of Britain fitted with a Benelux 4-speed derailleur gear. After trying different routes, inland and the coast, I settled for the following: Seaton Delaval, past the Keel Row, down the Laverock Hall road through Newsham, over the first railway gate to Newsham Road then on past the council yards to the North Farm pub, dropping off at the corner to reach the colliery Time Office.

I enjoyed the travelling to and from Bates Colliery. The rain and wind was no problem but sometimes the snow and ice made the journeys difficult and can recall many uncomfortable and hazardous trips. One such journey I remember vividly; it happened in 1969.

I was starting at 8am with a 4pm finish. Snow had been falling quite heavily before this particula morning but the roads were reasonably clear and cycling was not too bad. But thick snow had gathered in the fields on either side of the route. I clocked on at 10 minutes to 8 to relieve the foreshift man. During the morning the wind rose to a gale and continued all afternoon. I clocked off at 4pm and proceeded on the homeward journey.

I crossed the Newsham railway line then met a group of council workmen standing at the Laverock Hall turning. The conversation went something like this:

Workman: Where are you going?

Me: Up the Laverock to Seaton Delaval.

Workman: You'll never get up there. The road's blocked halfway.

Me: I came down this morning and it was OK then.

Workman: Suit yourself! But you're wasting your time.

The gales had apparently drifted the snow from the left-hand fields and covered the road. "Well I'm going up" I told them, and off I went. Not too bad really, I thought, as I crossed the colliery railway line that led to New Delaval Pit away on my right. Beyond there was a right sharp right-hand turn in the road and then, almost immediately, a left-hand turn. It was here, right in front of me, a wall of snow about 4 feet high - from the hedge on the left to the hedge on the right. I gazed in amazement. The council workers had cleared the road of snow to this point and that was that!

After I got over the shock, I hoisted my bike over the right-hand hedge and scrambled after it. Then with the cross bar over my shoulder I ploughed my way through the snow for fifteen or so paces and reached a point in the field where the depth of snow was reduced to an inch or two. I proceeded up the mile-long hill in the direction of the top road and the roundabout. The sky was still fairly light as I plodded along. I was not far from the top when I saw a van coming down the 'Laverock' from the roundabout. The road must be clear I thought, so I made my way left to join the road again. Nearing the hedge I looked over the top and watched the van come to a sudden stop. As I reached the hedge the driver was gazing out of the door. The van's front end was stuck fast in the wall of snow. He realised he could go neither forward or back. He was in a hell of a temper. "I was told this road was clear." he fumed. So I said "Now you know it's not." The time was now well after 5 o'clock and he was still there the next day as far as I know...

From there, with great caution, I arrived home half-an-hour later, much to the relief of my wife.

Tom 'Tot' Allan Seaton Delaval

Footpath to Rocky Island

ALL IN THE GAME...

Blue Star

On a Wednesday night I get dressed for football practice. With my hat, gloves and warm clothes on, I step out of the door, excited at what is going to happen. When I arrive I pick up a ball and start to kick it around, as you do.

Geoff, Hughie, Billy and Don come over and talk about Sunday's game. We start with a run, then do some ball work, have a few sprints then practice skills. At the end of the night we play a game. This is when the managers tell us what we're doing wrong. On the sidelines, the parents tell us what we're doing right.

Afterwards I get in the group for the team talk and listen to when we should meet on Sunday for the kick off.

The morning comes and I am raring to go. With the grass all green and also very wet we kick off.

But to my dismay, at the end of the day, we have lost 7-0.

Simon Adams (Age 11)

St Peter's Middle School, Cramlington

> Three referees were sent off during a referee's 5-aside competition. The dismissals followed a scuffle over a disputed penalty decision in the crucial Cramlington v. Newcastle match which decided regional winners [*January 1978*]

Seaton Delaval Amateurs. Twice Mayor of Blyth Valley, Jim Clough is seated (front far right)   Tom Allan Collectio

Me and my friends play football there.
We put our coats down for goal posts and have a game.
It isn't very good to play on but it's still a special place.
I don't know why, maybe it's because it belongs to us.
We argue if goals go in.
"'Course it did!"
"Spooner!"
"Get away with you!"
But we don't care.
At the end we're battered and bruised yet we'll be back tomorrow.
Sometimes we pretend it's the World Cup Final there.
A perfect setting for me.
Who will win?
The winner takes all.
Then the ball hits a bump
And goes a mile wide!

David Southern (Age 12)
St Peter's Middle School,
Cramlington

Blyth Spartans went down 2-1 to Murton. The deciding goal was deflected into the net by a dog which ran across the goal area. [*December 1947*] Blyth Spartans introduced their floodlights when they played Whitley Bay attracting 2,000 spectators [*October 1966*]

Mrs Elizabeth Waddle, a supporter of Blyth Spartans for 93 years, dies at the age of 105. [*February 1985*]

Spartans

I have been a supporter of Blyth Spartans for years; in fact I am a fanatic. I am a totally different person when I watch them. This dedication led to one of the most traumatic experiences of my life.

During my National Service I was stationed at Didcot, which was then in Berkshire. Most Fridays (except when you were on guard duty) you could get a 48-hour pass. We finished at the depot at 4pm and it was a dash to get the 4:30 train to Paddington Station. To improve our chances of catching the train we used to put our civilian clothes on under our uniform and then quickly throw off the top layer back at camp. In the summer we never had any bother getting a seat, I wonder why?

Blyth Spartans were at home one Saturday and I raced for the Paddington train then changed for Kings Cross to get the Newcastle connection. At the Central I caught the last train to Whitley Bay and walked all the way to Blyth reaching home at 5:30am. I told you I was a fanatic!

In the afternoon I saw the match. I forget the score so they must have won. I travelled back on the Sunday and got to Didcot at 6am on Monday ready to start work at 7:30am. I was shattered and looking forward to an early night. Unfortunately a deserter had been placed in custody at the camp and he was due at Colchester military prison next day. Extra guards were needed and I was chosen. So I found myself sitting in the guardroom with the guard commander and the prisoner at 11 o'clock at night. I was dead beat.

One of the cells was open so I took the opportunity to have a quick lie down and a quiet nap, so I thought. The next thing I knew, someone was prodding me with a swagger stick and ranting and raving. It was the orderly officer. He had been patrolling the camp and he had knocked on the guardroom door. It was opened by our prisoner. The guard commander had also fallen asleep in the chair. All hell broke loose! Anyone who has been in military service will appreciate the magnitude of our crime.

The following morning I was marched before the Regimental Sergeant Major, the Company Commander and finally the Battalion Commander; all of them were screaming and shouting their heads off. They demanded to know the reason for such negligence so I told them the truth, that I was tired after watching the Spartans play. They didn't seem to have any answer to that. They gave me a funny look and went quiet.

I got a severe warning about my future conduct but by then I had only a few weeks left to serve and then I would be back at Croft Park, when it would be my turn to do the screaming and shouting.

When I watch the Spartans there is no quarter asked or given. I go to see them win, nothing else matters. If they play badly for eighty-nine minutes and score in the last seconds to win, I am a happy man. I hate losing.

During the 1978 cup run I travelled down to Stoke with a very bad cold. When we got there the match was called off due to heavy snow and terrible wet conditions. By the time I got back to Blyth I was ill. I was actually off work for six weeks with a form of pneumonia. I was feeling a little better when the famous replay against Wrexham was due to take place. I ended up in the doctor's surgery pleading with him to give me some extra tablets so I could watch and survive the match. I was among the 42,000 who were at St James' Park. What a night!

Eddie Cain Blyth

Spartans Cup Team 1978

The Last Kick

After Blyth beat the second division team Stoke City 3-2, they drew 1-1 at Wrexham where the weather was atrocious. That Saturday most of the games were called off so Spartans dominated BBC's 'Match of the Day' and they even played our 'Zippedy-do-dah' anthem on the closing credits. We were leading 1-0 into injury time and even now I haven't come to terms with the way victory was snatched away from us. To start with, the referee gave them a corner in injury time, which was clearly a goal kick. Then incredibly the referee effectively penalised Spartans because the Wrexham player took the corner flag out! He made him take the kick again after Clarke, our goalie, had caught it. The winger put the flag back and they equalised from the second corner - unbelievable! The TV pundits said it was a dreadful decision. To put it into perspective, if Spartans had beaten Wrexham, they would have been only two wins away from the FA Cup Final at Wembley! Mind you they would have had to play Arsenal in the next round. But anything seemed possible. I wrote this after the replay at St James' Park where we lost 2-1. It's a little bit over the top, but it's how we felt all those years ago.

BLYTH SPIRIT

The 27th February in 1978
Was the day the English nation
Wondered what would be the fate
Of eleven local Geordies
Who were leaving work to drive
To meet the forty thousand
They were SPARTANS OF BLYTH.

St James' Park was bursting
They had to close the doors
Twelve thousand fans were left outside
To listen to the roars
The noise had reached crescendo
When we saw the lads arrive
The Leazes end was green and white
For the SPARTANS OF BLYTH

But not long after kick-off
Wrexham went ahead
It was a doubtful penalty
'Least that's what Scottie said.
Yet worse was still to follow
With Dixie's deadly drive
Which would have sunk a lesser team -
Not SPARTANS OF BLYTH

The crowd were right behind them
Slane's Army swept upfield
And free-kick followed corner
But Wrexham wouldn't yield
And even after half-time
Their spirits didn't dive
They drove themselves relentlessly

The SPARTANS OF BLYTH
The display of non-league courage
Was an awe-inspiring sight
Like the Ancient Greeks of Sparta
They were Geordies bred to fight.
With skill, determination
How did the Welsh survive?
They gave each ounce of effort
For the SPARTANS OF BLYTH

When Terry Johnson scored his goal
The whole of Tyneside cheered
Though visions of another 'Stoke'
Soon quickly disappeared
Six minutes saved the Welshmen
But we'd seen our players strive
With a truly moral victory
For the SPARTANS OF BLYTH

Emotion filled St James'
As the Spartans came around
To perform a lap of honour
And no-one left the ground.
We saw a piece of history
And I can't express my pride
For those eleven heroes
Who are SPARTANS OF BLYTH

The FA Cup continues
Without our non-league side
Yet those moments are remembered
For they earned much more than pride
All the country watched their progress
And the nation's now alive
To a new phrase meaning courage
It is SPARTANS OF BLYTH

Bill Blyth

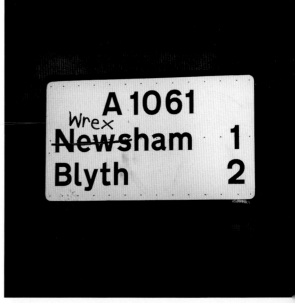

Blyth met Wrexham once again in the Debenham Cup that same season. The trophy was played for by the teams outside the top two divisions that had made the most progress in the F A Cup. It proved to be a triumph for Spartans as they won on Welsh soil. A jubilant returning fan displayed the score with some creative graffiti at the top of the Laverock Hall Road.

Blyth Spartans lost their replay against Bishop Auckland in the first round proper of the FA Cup after a record seven hours of play. [*December 1966*]

Spartans held Preston North End, with superstars Bobby Charlton and Nobby Stiles, to a 1-1 draw in the first round of the FA Cup. They lost the replay 5-1. [*November 1974*]

Croft Park

For those at the next match, and the people of Blyth:

I sit in the old concrete stand at the east side of Croft Park. It's Saturday afternoon in winter, it's cold, it's wet, it's dark.

Behind me, three old men sit silent, waiting for the game to start.

Then kick off. The loudest one, seizing control, is off like a dart:

BILL: (loudly) Wey it's too tight man, wa' not movin' it!

TOM: Aye, wa' not movin' it.

BILL: Thas' aboot seventy-five playas' on the pitch!

TOM: Aye, seventy-five playas'

BILL: Thas' more yelle' shirts than greens!

TOM: Aye, thas' more yelles' like.

Alf sits detached, munching boiled sweets and facing forward with a vacant stare.

He's not watching the game and not paying attention to the other pair.

BILL: (very loudly) Thas' nee' vision man!

TOM: Aye, thas' nee' vision.

BILL: (to Alf) Ya' quiet Alf, am' sayin to Tom that thas' nee' vision.

ALF: Eh?

BILL: Thas' nee' vision!

ALF: Eh?

BILL: Thas' nee' vision!!

ALF: Aah! Aye, Tuesday morning Bill.

(pause)

BILL: What?

TOM: What?

ALF: Eh?

I turn to my friend and laugh, but he's engrossed in the game. A saddened groan goes round the ground as a chance is missed again:

BILL: (loudly) Wey' that's another chance missed!

TOM: Aye, another one.

BILL: It's terrible!

TOM: Shockin'!

ALF: Eh?

BILL: It's Pyle man, he's too old. He's lost his pace. Av' always sed' see.

TOM: Aye, you have, like

The ball is pushed wide

then back inside. And hit.

Goal! Steve Pyle from thirty yards:

BILL: (louder still) Great goal by Pyle. FANTASTIC! Hav'nt a' always sed' see.

TOM: Aye you have like. He's fantastic!

'Tony' clambers up the steps but the crowd all dive for cover.

For when he speaks, he spits out pastie, huge chunks fly all over!

Sometimes though, my mate and I stand behind the nets with the younger blokes.

The conversation is often better than the match; sly comments, mad chanting, crude jokes:

"Ref ya' useless!"

[sung] "Ooh, Aah, Pyla. Ooh, Aah, Pyla!

"Howay Blyth, let's keep it going!î

[sung] "Keepa' Keepa', what's the score?"

"Spar-tans! Spar-tans!"

[sung] "Green, green, green and white army"

"Great! Wiv' scored, shite, so have they!"

[sung] "Wa' on wa' way to Wembley!"

[sung] "You'll neva' walk alone!"

Yet here at Croft Park, among all the characters, a match is played. And a small section of Blyth, even with its problems, is portrayed:

BILL: Wey it's these yelles, thav got nee spirit in tha game.

TOM: Nee spirit. At least Blyth's got spirit. Tha playin with passion.

BILL: You've said it there Tom, passion. That's Blyth through 'n' through.

         What d'ye think Alf? Alf?

ALF: Eh? Did ya' say sumic' Bill?

Andrew Steadman

Sixth Form, Blyth Ridley High School

Kevin Keegan, Liverpool and England striker, needed a police bodyguard when he visited Presto's Supermarket in Blyth due to an over enthusiastic welcome by fans. [*January 1977*]
Ray Kennedy of Seaton Delaval helps Arsenal win the League and Cup Double. [*May 1971*]

Alan Shearer scores a hat-trick for Cramlington Juniors Under-16's in their 7-0 victory against rivals New Hartley in the NFA Junior Cup [*January 1986*]
Andy Sinton, 14 year old Cramlington schoolboy footballer, has been picked for the England Under-15 team that meet Northern Ireland at Wembley Stadium. [*March 1981*]

Football [1950]

I often played football with the lads from the Bella. The games took place behind the colliery houses between the backyards and the coalhouse toilet blocks. Since they were close to home, no-one had jackets to put down for posts, so a couple of tin baths were taken from their rusty nails in the yard, stood on end, and used for goals. Not many kids had leather 'casers' so it was always tennis balls that we kicked around. If we hit the baths there would be quite a clatter; no-one could dispute a goal when the lane rang out with direct hits. We even called a goal a 'rowdie'! So the final score might be 'five rowdies to three.'

Brian Watson Blyth

Ray Kennnedy returns to Bates Welfare for a schoolboy presentation in 1973

World snooker champion Steve Davis was in Blyth to hand over the keys of a mini bus for handicapped children to the Borough Mayoress Mrs Elizabeth Collier. [*April 1984*]

Dart's champion, Eric Bristow, took on local opposition at the Spartan Hotel, Blyth, in front of eighty spectators [*March 1978*]

Dad [Extract]

Whilst I have happy memories of Dad there were a few I could have done without. He was a very good swimmer and diver and had received various medals and awards. I was terrified of the water when I was small but tried not to show it. I can put this down to the fact that every summer for as long as I can remember we spent a lot of time on the beach. Dad was a member of the swimming club and the families used to congregate between the piers, complete with swimming suits and picnic meals. I hated it. I was shy and was FRIGHTENED OF WATER. The adults used to go off to swim and the children were left playing on the sand. I used to watch Mam and Dad go off. One minute they were there; the next I could not see them. I felt so frightened, I thought they had gone forever. Even though they returned each time, this did nothing to quell my fear. I dared not say anything for Dad would have been disgusted at me showing him up. No amount of persuasion on his, or anyone else's part, would induce me to learn to swim. I know this was a big disappointment to him.

Dorothy Redpath Blyth

The Queen and the Prince Philip, in their Silver Jubilee year, visited Cramlington High School and opened the £2m Concordia Leisure Centre [*July 1977*]

Blyth's £1.75m Sports Centre was opened by John Ryman MP. [September 1979]
Dennis Lillee, the Australian fast bowler, came to Cramlington to help launch Concordia Leisure Centre's first family fun day. [*July 1981*]

Swimming Baths At Concordia

We go to the swimming baths to have fun on the slides and the big polystyrene floats. Sometimes we have fun-fights over them but that's alright. The lifeguard blows his whistle and you break it up and go your separate way. The buzzer goes and you get out and step into the cooler air. It is good under the hot shower with your towel by your side. But you never get rid of the chlorine smell.

Sarah Wood (Age 11)

St Peter's Middle School,
Cramlington

After being open for only eight months, Blyth Swimming Bath's 250,000th customer 'took the plunge' [*January 1968*]
Blyth Lifeguard and Swimming Club closed its membership until January when the figure reached 1200. [*October 1968*]

Sharon Davis, the Olympic silver medallist, makes her first visit to the North to swim in a competition at Blyth Sports Centre. [*November 1980*]

Baywatch?
Blyth Lifeguard Club
1966

Humford Pool [1954]

I learnt to swim at the open-air Humford Woods bathing pool. My dad took me there and three things are still vivid in my memory. Firstly, there were the cramped wooden changing cubicles that stood like sentry boxes at the side of the pool; for some reason they made me nervous. Secondly, I was surprised to discover the pool wasn't salty and that the river water was warmer than the sea. The most memorable feature was the surface of the water which was covered with dead insects. There were very few swimming pools in the area so you couldn't be choosy. I suspect I was so terrified of swallowing the floating flies that I kept my head clear of the water.. and swam my first strokes.

Forty years on, there is a paddling pool and climbing frames where the swimming pool used to be. When the sun shines the families come out, and once again it is a busy, cheerful spot.

Bill Blyth

Blyth Valley send a defiant British Olympic team £100 of the defunct lottery fund to help them on their way to Moscow. [*June 1980*]

Six youngsters from Centre 64 set up a world record of non-stop table tennis for 101 hours. [*January 1967*]

Seaton Sluice student, Steven Higgins, was chosen to cox for Oxford against Cambridge in the 129th boat race [*February 1983*]

A million to one chance came off on Captain's Day at Blyth Golf Club when Alan Jamieson took a hole in on one at the 9th with a repeat performance by Jim Rowly at the 2nd - 5 minutes later. [*July 1986*]

Spence of Blyth' winning the 1947 Powderhall

Spence Of Blyth

In 1946, Albert Grant, a Blyth submariner, came back from the 'Med', entered a running race at Burradon, and won. In post-War summer months there were foot-races at all the local flower shows and professional sprinters would compete for prize money of up to £100. They could increase their earnings by betting on themselves; the higher the odds the better the pay-day.

Promising runners were whisked away by sponsors who would pay a retainer to the athlete in return for being handled by their 'school'. This would involve secret training, special diet and a honing of the runner's fitness until the 'wraps' could be removed and their little-known protege could get a good mark (a few yards start) and good odds at a significant race meeting.

Albert's talent was spotted early and nurtured. His name was changed to Spence - his mother's maiden name. This was a common practice to disguise the true identity of the runner. Albert was given a 'prep' (preparation) at Silloth in Cumbria for the major event on the pro's calender: 'The Powderhall'. This world famous race took place in Edinburgh.

On New Years' Day, 1947, Spence of Blyth won his heats in the 100-yard event and later in the afternoon, in appalling weather, he surprised everyone, except himself and his backers, by winning the championship. The odds were high and the story goes that the school left an Edinburgh hotel with all their winnings wrapped up in a bed sheet! This was the beginning of Albert's spectacular running career.

In the London Olympics of 1948, Britain's McDonald Bailey was just behind the winner. Albert throughout the year had been running a yard quicker on the same tracks as Bailey but as a professional sprinter he was barred from the amateur games. Albert could have won gold, he was that good!

Eighteen months later in an all-expenses-paid trip, he was invited to run in Australia in a series of races that were billed as the 'World Championship' and it included USA's Barney Ewell, the Olympic silver medallist and generally accepted to be the fastest man on earth. The long journey by sea left Albert ill-prepared but by the end of the series the Blyth runner recorded 10.93 seconds for a world-best time over 110 yards.. on grass! On his return he gave up his painter and decorator job on the Blyth council building sites and opened up a physiotherapy shop with his winnings.

For ten years Albert remained unbeaten in this country off a 'scratch' mark. At the official opening of the new floodlights at Arsenal's Highbury stadium, Albert won the professional sprint title in front of a crowd of 60,000. 'Spence of Blyth' won it again the following year. The people of the town remember his exhibition runs at Croft Park when thousands turned up to watch him break his own British record.

Eye-Witness

I walked over to Croft Park to see him race and I often think about that day. After months in Australia, Albert's blond hair was bleached with the sun and his body was all bronzed, I mean in Blyth most of the men worked down the pit or in the shipyards, so you hardly ever saw a sun-tan. Albert had star quality in his pure white track suit with 'Spence of Blyth' in bold red letters. He wasn't a big man but he was perfectly muscled.. just like a Greek God, I thought.

I watched from the back of the stand as he warmed up on his own, stretching his legs and striding out. There were heats being run but every eye was on Albert. He wasn't aloof, he was just preparing.. and everyone kept a respectful distance.

There was total silence as he took his mark and after the gun, he sprang from his blocks, and me and the other ten thousand spectators just stared in disbelief at the sheer speed of his legs. He skimmed over the grass. I had no idea anyone could run that fast. I was so proud that Albert came from Blyth, but it was scary too, because I knew without a doubt, he really was a gift from the Gods.

[Extract from the play 'Pro's and Cons']

Back home, he started Blyth Athletics Club and coached two subsequent

Albert 'Spence' Grant (left) with Blyth runners Gerry Evans (centre) and Joe Ball (right) Joe won the 1957 Powderhall

winners of the Powderhall; his son Carl was twice a finalist too. Albert Grant used his reputation to persuade the council to build a cinder running track in the town and it was here that he would train and encourage youngsters, long after his own competitive days were over.

The club had considerable success until he fell foul of the Amateur Athletic Association who took a dim view of pro's training on the same track as their 'pure' amateur runners. In spite of Albert's enormous contribution to the sport, officials were on the look-out for infringements of their code of practice.

In 1976 the club took some athletes to a low key event in Cumbria where Blyth youngsters won the sprints. They expected trophies but there was considerable concern when a winner was handed a 50p piece. Immediately Albert withdrew his runners from the proceedings as the Blyth competitors had unknowingly taken part in a professional meeting where money was awarded and not prizes. Had the prize have been a £200 washing machine (not uncommon in top amateur races) then this would not have contravened the AAA's regulations.

At the British Athletics Federation half Marathon Championships during the 1993 Great North Run, Blyth Running Club's ladies were the National Champions. Gill Priest (L) Sheila Greener (centre) and Cath Coultate (R) made up the successful team

Although other local amateur runners had also been misled, it was Albert who was reported to the AAA's administrators and was subsequently banned from coaching, as it was considered he was 'a bad influence' on young people.

Blyth A.C. owed their existence to Albert's tireless efforts. He withdrew from the committee in order to spare the club embarrassment but the members unanimously decided that without Albert they no longer wished to be a part of the athletics establishment and the club disbanded on the spot.

The first Concordia to Blyth Sports Centre run in 1982

Albert 'Spence' Grant was a magnificent world-class athlete, respected by his opponents, and admired by those who knew him. He died within the year of the ban. He still enjoyed his life to the full but a close friend maintained it was the '50p-business that killed him'.

Andy Griffin Blyth.

FOOTNOTE

Funds from Albert's old athletic club were transferred to Blyth Running Club six years after they disbanded when the Great North Run produced a new generation of athletes. Blyth RC now has a membership of over two-hundred and in 1987 was voted into second place in a national 'Running Club of the Year' Award.

More than 400 enthusiasts, including the Mayor of Blyth Jim Clough, took part in the Borough's first fun run. [*April 1982*]

WORKING ON THE RAILWAY...

I worked on the railway for the Hartley Main Collieries and the National Coal Board from 1935 to 1960.

When steam engines 'ruled' in the 20's and 30's it was said that every schoolboys' dream was to be an engine-driver. I never had such dreams and for most of the young lads who left school at the age of fourteen any sort of job was welcome in 1932.

I became an errand boy at a local boot and shoe shop in Seaton Delaval which did repairs at the rear of the building. The wage was seven shillings (35p); later with an increase of sixpence (2¹/₂p) making a total of 'seven and six' a week. I occasionally had the use of a free pass to the local Queens Hall Cinema because of a display notice in the shop window.

After a year I answered an advertisement in a local paper for a job at F Bell's Nursery Gardens behind Whitley Bay railway station. This was hard work earning fifteen shillings (75p) per week although sometimes during the summer months I could make up to £1 with overtime. I liked the work very much and had to travel to Whitley Bay on my bicycle every day (except Sunday) to start at 8 am. Many young women used the same mode of transport for going into service or 'to place' as maids for the more well-off residents of Whitley Bay.

When I was just over 17 years of age my Uncle Jack, who worked at the Seaton Delaval Colliery as an engine-driver, asked me if I would like to work on the 'tankies' at the colliery. This led to a successful interview with the Engineer at the colliery yard and I gave a week's notice at the nurseries. The next Saturday was my last day and the Engineer told me to start the following night at 10.30pm. Seventeen years of age and straight into a night shift job starting on Sunday night! This was entirely different to my day-time work.

However, I 'clocked on' at the time office and strolled around to the loco-shed which was to be my depot for a year. I learnt that the other lad working there was Edgar, an old school pal. There was also an older man named George, who was the night-shift shed foreman. I saw immediately that he only had one hand (right) and his left hand was replaced by a crook (compensation man)

Loco Sheds at Seaton Delaval Colliery Disused in 1978

The working environment was grim. It was dimly lit and everywhere seemed to be dirty with smoke and soot. There were eight or nine engines inside the shed and one or two standing outside. They all had to be 'lit up' and steamed for various times during the early hours of Monday morning. The crews (drivers, firemen) and guards had to start work according to a time-sheet which was pinned on a door in the shed.

The most important job Edgar and I had to do was 'calling out' or 'knocking up'. The crews for the locos had to be called out in the early hours of Monday morning. Edgar had been working at the depot for some months and he showed me how to go on. For the first few nights we both left the loco-shed to call the men about an hour before their starting times. Some lived at New Hartley and others at Seaton Delaval. Several men worked at the Cramlington side which was also Hartley Main Collieries. After a while I was on my own - doing New Hartley one week and Seaton Delaval the next. I found it most enjoyable cycling round the district especially on a moonlit night when all was quiet and nobody to be seen. I really liked it!

One house I had to go to was in Melton Terrace, New Hartley, to call out Will, a Cramlington driver. I'd knock on the back-door, then step back into the lane so I could see the roof with the sky-light window. Within a few seconds the window would open and a face in the gloom would say "Aye lad?" I would reply with his time for starting and maybe tell him if he was on a long shift so he could take extra bait. "Righto" he would answer and that was that. In the meantime, back at the loco-shed, the fires were being started in the engines. This was done by a regular engineman who came in on the Sunday night for this purpose. He would place paraffin-soaked cotton waste on the bars of the fire-box, and after lighting this, sticks were placed on the fire then coals (bunkers) were shovelled on.

Loco 21 at Water Tank, Percy Main   Tom Allan Collection

If the engine's chimney was under the smoke-stack, it was OK, the smoke poured out into the skies; but if not, the smoke accumulated inside the loco-shed until you could not see a hand in front of you. On these occasions we were forced outside into the night air. Sometimes when the smoke filled the rafters we would hear a 'plop' on the shed floor. That would be a sparrow, overcome with fumes, dropping from its perch.

My first Sunday night passed over quickly and at about 6:30am we prepared for 'off'. Our hands were filthy! A short piece of rail, about six inches long (15cm) was tossed into the huge sand-drying fire. When it was red hot it was dropped into a bucket of cold water to heat it up. The soft soap then did the trick of cleaning. But what about George the foreman's hand? Another one of our jobs. Edgar and I took it in turns to wash and dry his good hand. The crook on his left arm came in handy when he was chopping the wood blocks into sticks for 'lighting up'. He held the block of wood with his crook and used the axe in his good hand to slice the wood. If the axe slipped and caught his crook - no harm done!

My first night was over and at 7am we clocked off and headed for home. Sleep was not easy in the day time. Monday evening soon came round and at 10:30pm it was back to the loco-shed once more.

The sand-drying fire was stirred up and its roaring furnace made the place more comfortable. The 'calling out' had to be done again and the starting sheet pinned to the door. The engines outside would come in after cleaning their fires out on the shed bank just outside the loco-shed. The sand boxes of the engine had to be filled up with dry sand. It was our job to carry pails of sand to the fireman who filled the boxes.

Tom eating his Bait 1940

With a sand-box on either side of the smoke box (front end) and two in the cab, or fixed on the frame either side of the cab (back end), there were quite a few pails to carry. The sand was used when the rails were dampened by rain or early morning dew, resulting in the driving wheels losing traction and causing 'slipping'. The sand was gravity fed by levers operated in the cab and they allowed sand to fall onto the rail surface so the wheels could grip and provide motion for the loco. During the shift Edgar and I also had to riddle dry sand into a large brick storage container. Having done that, more wet sand was shovelled out of a nearby sand pit onto the hot plate to dry for the next day.

During the week we had to 'light up' the one or two engines which were in the loco shed when we started at 10:30pm. These fires were easily started with a shovel of red fire from the sand-drying furnace. It was placed on the box bars and covered with coal (bunkers) and that was that!

It was warm place to work and the drivers would come into our shed for a chat and a cup of tea round a roaring fire; there was never any shortage of coal. Some of the crews carried square Johnny Walker whiskey bottles which they filled with tea (without milk - it curdled) and they would stand them on the shelf at the boiler end, or on the floor, so that they would heat up during their shift. The square edges stopped their bottle from rolling about. We used the sand beds for the same purpose.

One morning my Uncle Jack asked me if I would like to go with him on a trip to the River Tyne after finishing at 7am. This was my first experience of watching a fireman firing a loco.

The 7-mile [11km] route to the River Tyne was on the private line of the Hartley Main Collieries and to arrive at the staithes at Percy Main, it ran over the tracks of L.N.E.R. [London & North Eastern Railways - later British Rail] Beginning at Seaton Delaval the journey took in Seghill, then through Holywell Gates, Earsdon Junction and the Blue Bell gates at Shiremoor. Soon after this point the going was downhill all the way to Percy Main with gradients of 1 in 50 in places. It was necessary to pin down two or three of the brakes on the twenty 10-ton coal wagons. At Percy Main our load was uncoupled and lined up ready to be shipped out of the Tyne. For the return journey we picked up a train of 30 empty wagons and reached our starting point at Seaton Delaval Colliery after a two hour round trip. It was quite exciting work!

Gradually I got used to the unsocial hours and I was on my way to being an engine driver. At 18 years of age I was allowed to go outside as a guard - shunting and marshalling the loaded sets of wagons for engines going to the staithes. After 12 years I became a permanent fireman. I had by now started shifts on every hour and almost every half-hour around the 24-hour clock. I finally became an engine-driver in 1954.

Rumours began circulating of pit closures in the early 1950's. I did five years driving when the situation began to look desperate. Enginemen were finished and I was demoted back to firing. In 1960 the pit closed. It was an end to twenty-five years of interesting and enjoyable work on the engines of the Hartley Main Collieries Ltd (later the NCB).

I was transferred to Bates Pit, Blyth; worked on the locos for a short time then was transferred to a newly built boiler-house - raising steam for the heating of baths and surface buildings. I was on a three-shift system. During the five-month period of winter, we worked continuously through week-ends. This meant for me, sixteen-hour shifts over Saturday and Sunday.

Twenty-one years later at the age of 62 I took voluntary redundancy. Bates Colliery closed in February 1986 by which time I was on my pension.

Tom 'Tot' Allan Seaton Delaval

Tom Allan Collection

A platelaying team at New Hartley

Dissatisfaction is caused as the daily railway service from Blyth to Newcastle is cut from 23 trains to 14 [later restored] [*March 1950*]

Dad [Extract]

Most of his working life Dad worked as a platelayer for London and North Eastern Railway and was known to be a very energetic and conscientious worker. He was a kind man, a real rough diamond, but always thinking of others. In those days the wages were very meagre for most people and often things were tight for working families. When the 'gang' were replacing sleepers on the track, the gaffers would tell the men to bury or burn the old ones. When this happened near home, Dad, being a law unto himself, chose to ignore this instruction. He did not see why the families should not benefit from having some wood to burn to help eke out the coal which had to be bought. Dad would use his great strength and drag some of the old timbers off and put them underneath the nearby signal cabin. Later, he would unearth his well-hidden old saw and cut the sleepers into manageable lengths. I remember seeing Dad and one of his workmates coming home at the end of the day carrying lumps of wood tied around with 'tarry tout' (creosoted rope). Throughout my life whenever I smell this, it reminds me of those happy, contented days.

Dorothy Redpath Blyth

British Railways announced its decision to operate a diesel passenger train service from Newcastle to East Northumberland to replace the old push-and-pull steam locomotives. [*December 1957*]
The first diesel passenger train left Blyth for Newbiggin. [*June 1958*]

Railway Station, Blyth

Flying Scotsman De-Railing

The Flying Scotsman 1973   Tom Allan Collection

I was ten years of age in 1926 when the General Strike began. The miners had demanded 'Not a penny off the pay, not a minute on the day'. They were supported by the TUC and a national strike was called. Five days after the start of the dispute the trains were being run again by blackleg staff. Managers and undergraduate students (playing out their fantasies as engine drivers) were operating the trains. Many railwaymen (not the drivers) were starting to drift back. A group of miners in the 'Box Eggs' pub in Cramlington decided to do something about it. They walked the short distance along the branch line to the main passenger line and chased away the plate-layers who were working there; the miners had had a drink remember. The railwaymen ran to Cramlington station to warn the incoming trains that there could be trouble ahead.

Meanwhile the eight miners broke into the plate-layers cabin, stole their tools, and disconnected two parallel lines, sixty feet in length. They removed the fish-plates that joined them together and knocked the chocks out of the 'shoes' so the rails were lying loose. Then they waited for the famous Flying Scotsman passenger train which always travelled between Cramlington and Annitsford each day, just after lunch.

The driver of the train had been stopped at the station and warned but he decided to continue slowly through the trouble spot. From his vantage point, as he passed through the cutting (and on the sharpest bend on the whole of the LNER network) he couldn't see a problem.. but he soon felt one! The engine slipped off the loose rails and keeled over on its side and ploughed through nearly 100 yards of ballast at the edge of the track. Two carriages behind were also pulled off the tracks. The volunteer fireman on the engine had his wrists scalded; that was the only injury. As usual on a Monday, the train was full of touring theatricals. They usually travelled back to London from Edinburgh after the week-end.

I was at Annitsford waiting for the bus to take me home from school when the news broke, so we had to see if it was true. Me, Jimmy Wrightson and Jimmy Durnan ran over there, and sure enough the Flying Scotsman was still on its side with steam pouring out. I remember the name of the engine, it was called the Merry Hampton. I tried to get a closer look and I squeezed between the train and the buffers but one of the officials gave me a clip! We stayed at the scene for hours.. we didn't notice the time. In those days nobody had watches, we got our time from the clocks in the street. Out there though, we lost track of time. I didn't get home until half-past eight.

I'll not forget the 10th May 1926 because there was two injured victims on that night; I was the second. I got such a belting from my Grandad. The family had been worried; there was always danger in the colliery villages from the ponds and railways. My Grandad by now was 88 but he gave me such a lathering, the one and only time he took his thick belt to me. The tears were running down my cheeks, and they were running down his as well. I'd never seen that before either.

They caught the miners. One of them turned King's Evidence and told on his mates. He got off with a light jail sentence and then disappeared without trace. The rest served eight to twelve years for their crime. If anyone had been killed on that day, the miners would have been hanged; no question about that.

The train lay abandoned for weeks. They actually put down another line alongside to skirt round the engine because the drivers were still on strike and they refused to shift it.

The nation was horrified at the incident but the miners were unrepentant and said they would have done it all over again; such was the strength of feeling during the General Strike. A rumour was put about that the miners were expecting coal wagons coming down the line from Pegswood and that they never meant to attack the Flying Scotsman, but that was nonsense. There was a strike on wasn't there? No coal was being moved.. anywhere! They knew what they were doing alright. These men were folk heroes at the time, and I tell you, there was quite a celebration at the Box Eggs pub when they were released from jail.

Arthur Heayns Klondyke

Embankment

Nine coal wagons were derailed at North Blyth staithes demolishing a bus shelter. [*August 1953*]

I attended Blyth Grammar School after passing the 11plus examination Each morning I walked across the open path at the end of Gordon Road and joined the steady stream heading for Plessey Road. We crossed the Newsham railway line over the footbridge that was always known locally as the 'green bridge'. Most of this area in the 50's and 60's to the south of Plessey Road was made up of open fields and ponds, with dirt tracks or cinder paths running through it all the way up to Blyth's 9-hole golf course behind Barrass Avenue. It was part of our school's testing cross country course; now it is South Beach Estate. Rotary Way was not built until the 1970's and the coastal route to Blyth was past the timber yards and the front of our house. Today, the old embankment that carried the railway line has now been landscaped but it can still be seen at right angles to Rotary Way as it runs behind Hunter Avenue. At this crossing there used to be a loading bay for the open cast coals. Lorries came by road to this point and tipped their load from a ramp into the trucks below. From here, there was just a short journey to the staithes and the waiting ships.

David Phillipson Tynemouth

The millionth ton of coal has been recovered in less than two years from the mammoth Acorn Bank opencast site near Bedlington. [*November 1957*]

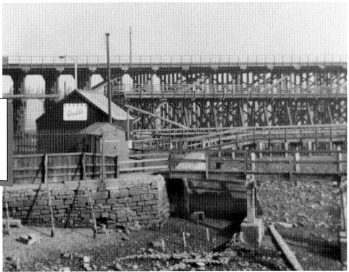

North Blyth Staithes near High Ferry

COAL CONCERTO
[Ridley Park Staithes]

Wobbly railway rhythms
Truckfulls of coal
Cornering
Skirling wheel rims
Squealing..

Disharmonious
bagpipe
tuning.

Brian Watson Cramlington

Representatives of 13 local authorities in the county met at Blyth to protest against the Beeching Plan to axe the railway passenger service from Newcastle to Blyth and Newsham. 182 objections are received from organisations and individuals but the cuts will take place in the new year. [*September 1963*]

Cramlington railway station, threatened with closure by British Railways, was given a reprieve. [*October 1965*]

Teeming

Crofton Mill Pit was near the town centre and I worked 'on bank' for a year then they sent me underground. I didn't take to it, too dark for my liking. I left the pit and got fixed up on the railways as a number taker which is a sort of outside clerk. I had to write down the 'numbers' or weight of the coal wagons to make sure they balanced with the figures that were recorded when they left the colliery.

I spent two of my happiest years there before being called up at nineteen for compulsory National Service in the army. Every young lad was called up (unless they had special exemption) and you could be sent all over the world to fight for your country.. and this was not long after the war. There was some dangerous places abroad and I was posted to one of them in Egypt. There was the Suez crisis at the time and we had to prepare to do battle with Nasser. The fighting was over before we had even left. We were relieved about that.

When I got back to Blyth I was lucky enough to get a job as a coal teemer for the railways in the River Blyth. It was good money but hard work. We had to load up the waiting colliers from the staithes. At the time Blyth was the biggest exporter of coal in the world. When we beat off the challenge from South Wales in 1963/64 we were shipping out over six million tons. There was a fair bit of jealousy and rivalry amongst the ports.

We had to get up at 4 o'clock in the morning for a 5 o'clock start. The summer months were not bad but the winter was terrible. Can you imagine working 60 feet above the ground on the exposed wooden staithes? When the snow was blowing and the west wind was up, it would cut you in two. But you had to be up there in all weathers because the coal was teemed into the boats through the gravity spouts.

A pilot engine pushed the wagons of coal to the buffers where we were waiting. One of the teemers would line them up over the hopper and put the breaks on and use a wooden chock to stop the wagons from sliding past the opening. If there was rain or snow we had to put sand

Loader, Blyth Staithes

on the rails to stop them slipping. Once in position, the pins holding the wagon doors (which were in the bottom of the tubs) were knocked away and the coal dropped out.

Teemers were thought to be well-paid because it was piece work and we could get through as many as 200 wagons a shift. But I have seen some days when we only teemed four wagons all morning. In winter the coal would freeze in the wagons and it had to be dug out by hand. Four wagons was approximately 80 tons and the normal teem would be 4,000 tons a shift! On the West Staithes I remember loading a 4,200 ton boat in less than eight hours.

There were teeming berths all over the River Blyth. The West Staithes had five teeming points and there were many more points at the North Staithes, South Cowpen and Bates Colliery. They have all closed over the years and most have been cut down. Bates is the last and sadly that's on its way out too.

Tommy Robertson Blyth

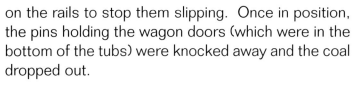

Teemers and trimmers on the River Blyth worked at full pressure to reduce the loading queue of twenty-one ships; caused by gales holding up the output. [*November 1956*]

A Day Out

A special day out when I was a child was a trip to Newcastle from Blyth. We could get the train to Monkseaton and link up with the coast circular line - now the Metro. My dad would take me to Woolworths for a coca-cola. It came in a chunky glass bottle and I drank it through a wax straw. Later we would go to the Tatler at the top of Northumberland Street and see the newsreels and the cartoons. You could stay there all day. When people went to the pictures they never bothered with the starting times because the films ran continuously so you just watched until it came round again. Halfway through a film you would hear people whisper 'This is where we came in' and they might get up and go, or just as likely they would sit through it a second time.

After the pictures my dad would take me to the Newcastle Central station and I would spend thru'pence on this big red cast iron machine. It had a sort of a clock face with a heavy brass pointer and all the way around there were letters of the alphabet and numbers from one to ten. What you did, was to choose a letter with the pointer then pull down a lever (a bit like a one-armed bandit) and that punched the letter onto a thin narrow strip of metal. You were allowed twenty-one pulls and you could spell out your name or your address. It was really exciting when your 'label' came out. I did what most of the kids used to do, and that was bend it round my wrist like a bracelet. It took off layers of skin but nothing would stop me from wearing it.

Mick Davison Station House, Blyth

Blyth Railway Station is pulled down after standing derelict for eight years [*February 1972*] (now the site of Safeways)

Christopher Clark

The last railway line leads to the Alcan hoppers on the North Pier.
Christopher Clark (Age 8) Blyth Kingsway First School 1995

THAT'S ENTERTAINMENT...

Wallaw

I love going to the pictures, but not when kids are there.

I consider kids in any cinema a pain.

When I went to see 'Mrs Doubtfire' I stupidly sat in the front row. As the film was a PG, the theatre was full of kids and as a consequence I spent most of the time removing popcorn from my hair, coat and lap!

At any early evening family show there are hoards of them.

I went to see 'Jurassic Park' at half-seven one time and I was driven half mad by the little monsters.. and not the ones on the screen!

From the start a little boy and a little girl chanted behind me:

"Mummy I'm bored, Mummy I want a drink, Mummy can I have some popcorn? Mummy I need the toilet" (they went four times in fifteen minutes).

And worst of all, over and over again:

"Mummy where are the dinosaurs?"

Finally, when the tyrannosaurus burst onto the screen roaring and snarling, there came a pathetic wailing:

"Mummy I don't like the noise!"

Kids, they're never satisfied.

Speaking of 'Jurassic Park', I've seen it twelve times and five of those visits were to the Wallaw. I was so impressed with the dinosaurs. They were, without doubt, the best thing about the film.

I once went to the Wallaw with eight other friends to see 'Star Trek; Generations'. I found it really boring but everyone else seemed to be enjoying it. They were clapping and cheering throughout. When we left the one who had been leading the applause announced:

"Well that was rubbish, wasn't it?"

Just before Christmas I went to see 'Babe'. I went with a couple of good friends and the film was very funny. It had been snowing outside and when we left the cinema I felt in a strangely good mood. I had really enjoyed myself.

I heard there was a danger of the Wallaw closing a while back and as I write I hope this risk has passed. The cinema has been a part of my life since I was very small and it holds so many memories for me. Blyth does not know what it has got in the Wallaw and it probably won't be appreciated until it has gone. I can't be the only one who hopes this never happens.

Blyth's last cinema, the Wallaw, closed down on December 18th because of poor support, only to re-open again eight days later when Mr Peter Cargill stepped in to take over the lease
[*December 1982*]

The Wallaw cinema became a theatre as Blyth Operatic Society staged 'Oklahoma'.
[*March 1967*]

Friends of the Wallaw

I consider the Wallaw as a part of Blyth that not many of us think about, but we all know it. The big old cinema must have been there long time. It is not a particularly impressive building; the bricks are a bit dirty. The posters in the plastic screens at the front are always wrinkled from the damp. The doorway is wide with a billboard to the right telling you what's on.

It's pretty smart inside; the lobby is large and clean-smelling. You pay on the left and there are stairways on both sides which you go up to the 'major'. Downstairs are the 'mini' and 'minor' screens. These two smaller theatres are not as old as the rest of the Wallaw.

I don't have a much spending money, so when I go to the Wallaw I tend to waddle in with a can of coke in my pocket, a bar of chocolate up my sleeve and a big bag of popcorn under my jumper. Being a total cheapskate, I spend most of my time in and around the Wallaw doing a pretty good impersonation of the Michelin Man.

I've been going there since I was a little kid. I went to see 'The Never-Ending Story' and was hysterical over the death of a horse. I was six. I also went to see 'The Land Before Time' and everyone cried when the baby dinosaur's mum died, except me. I sat and handed out the tissues. I always found crying over films a little bit pointless so it was highly humiliating, when at the age of fifteen, I went through a crying spree at every film I saw, including 'Lady and the Tramp' 'Aladdin' 'Free Willy' and 'The Lion King'.

There was a phase when I went to the pictures once a week with my sister Emma and her two friends, Lisa and Sarah (names have been changed to protect the guilty). Lisa and Sarah usually wore make-up to the pictures, even when they were only twelve. This caused problems when we went to see 'Edward Scissorhands'. At the end they cried bucketloads, I could hear the sobs from the toilet where I hid in shame. On emerging from the dark Lisa looked as though she had gone ten rounds with Frank Bruno, whilst Lisa resembled Chi-Chi the panda! I laughed all the way home.

It was with Lisa and Sarah that I endured my most embarrassing moment at the pictures. We had come to see 'The Lawn-mower Man' and we were late in. The lights were down and the film was running. We saw some spare seats in the front row but knew we had to keep our heads down to avoid getting in the way of the screen. We started jogging to our places. This was my first time in the 'minor' and I did not realise the little bit in front of the screen sloped forward and upwards. As I hurriedly reached this point, my foot caught the slope and the next thing I knew I was soaring across the screen and landing flat on my face in front of an astonished audience of about 25 people. The entire theatre laughed out loud and my friends pretended not to know me. I pulled my coat up over my head and virtually crawled to my seat where I sat so low down that it looked like I wasn't there at all. I wouldn't leave the cinema until everyone else had gone, then I limped home, nursing a sprained ankle and a bruised pride. At first I refused to return to the Wallaw but I was bullied back within a month.

Darkness has always caused me problems at the pictures.

Paula Sainthouse

Sixth Form, Blyth Ridley High School.

After a private showing of the controversial Monty Python film 'Life of Brian', Blyth Valley councillors agree to its screening in the town.
[*June 1980*]

Pictures

The Palace

Thirty years ago there were plenty of places to go to in Blyth if you fancied the 'pictures'. There was the Central, the Essoldo, the Wallaw and the Roxy and Theatre Royal showed films as well - not to mention Newsham. The Roxy is now the Bingo Hall by the bus station and the Wallaw is the last survivor, the rest have gone.

Mick Davison Blyth

One of Blyth's four picture halls, The Central, closes down as a cinema to begin life as the town's first full-time bingo hall. [*June 1961*]

Talkies

My mother worked for 18 years at the King George V Picture Hall in Klondyke. She started as an usherette and earned six shillings [30p] a week. She finished when I was twenty-one and her wages were still only eight shillings [40p]. I got to see all the pictures and I used to help the projectionist Mollie Lisle. Mollie would set the film going then nip off to the club on his little old two-stroke motor bike and forget about the projectors. Many's the time I've had to change the reel or fix the film when it broke.

The Central

When they changed the screen for the talkies they couldn't understand why the old one was full of little marks.. tiny holes that you could only see close up. I knew, so did Mollie. I had often been watching the cowboy pictures with him when he would get his air pistol out. He would shoot the baddies on the screen during the final chase on horseback. No-one in the cinema was any the wiser.

Arthur Heayns Klondyke

A cinemascope film can be enjoyed for as little as ninepence at Seghill Colliery Welfare cinema. [*November 1958*]

Tom Allan Collection

Queens Hall – Bingo ex Cinema. Sept 1991

Lucky Bags And Matinees

"Mam can I have a penny for a lucky bag and a penny for the pictures?"

Saturday morning. The matinee at the Queen's Hall Cinema was the high spot of the village children's lives.

"It's Tarzan of the Apes."

Ben happily informed his Mam.

"Can I go with Hylton and Tommy?"

Ben's Mam was glad that her husband had found some temporary work on the council's new housing estate. Yes, she could afford to let Ben go to the pictures.

The three lads ran down Astley Road to Alec Harper's sweet shop. It was only a house with a large window and the rooms were converted with shelves and counters. This shop was a wonderland, packed with large bottles of Welches Sweets. Jelly babies (bite their heads off first) gob stoppers, black bullets, sugar mice, mint imperials, barley sugars and many more. Paying for their lucky bag (a mixture of sweets) they ran to the Queen's and stood in line with children from the surrounding areas, to see their hero Tarzan. Mr Renny was the doorman and with the manager, Mr Carr, they kept control of the excited children. As usual, when the main film ended, the serial started. It was a long-running saga called 'The Mystery Riders'. All the children would sing to the theme tune:

"We are the Mystery Riders, we go to China to seek gold."

"See you later down the Avenue."

Hylton's cry was echoed by many youngsters. The Avenue was (and still is) a double-line of trees separated by a road. It had been the private drive to Seaton Delaval Hall and it was once protected by iron gates and two imposing pillars. Now the drive was open to the public and it led on to Seaton Sluice, Blyth and Whitley Bay. It was also a wonderful playground for children and a popular walk for their parents.

On this day, Ben ran home singing 'Mystery Riders' and slapped his side to make the horse go faster. The films were always re-enacted amongst these trees. Robin Hood, cowboys and indians, Tarzan, gangsters, wars and battles, all had their outings; brought to life by the relentless imagination of the children.

Tom Humphrey Seaton Sluice

Street Entertainment [1950's]

The first 'medieval' banquet was held at Lord Hasting's home at Seaton Delaval Hall.
[*March 1969*]

Blyth market place on a Saturday very often featured bare-chested sword-swallowers and fire-eaters. It amazed me that a man could run a fearful looking flame across his oily torso without being burnt alive. I recall the crowds that gathered when a member of the public was invited to tie up one of the performers, first with ropes, then with chains and padlocks. The challenge seemed impossible. But after an initial show of doubt, there would be much vigorous activity, followed by a movement resembling a speeded-up centipede, and the escapologist would be up on his feet with chains and ropes all around him. He would have a hat in his hand immediately, but, by magic, the crowd would perform their own disappearing act.

Circuses and fairs were a regular feature in the town after the war and in the summer months Big Top tents were erected either at Broadway field or near the beach by the Jubilee Cafe. There was usually a procession along the major roads in Blyth which always included our patch at Plessey Road and this advertising guaranteed a good turn-out. They stayed for a week and brought a very welcome diversion. Wafts of sound and music carried to our house in the long summer evenings and I can remember how the coloured lights came on as dusk descended. When the showmen left we could still see where their stalls and tents had stood because the grass beneath had dried to the colour of hay. We would scour the area in vain for dropped pennies or thru'penny bits amongst the trampled grass.

Brian Watson Cramlington

Cramlington's first carnival, opened by Newcastle United's John Tudor, declared a big hit [*June 1971*]

Blyth Carnival 1982

117

The Fair

"Have you heard about the new ride called the Apollo?"

Charlene questioned Helen as they were on their way to the fair.

"Yeah, from what I've heard it's supposed to be great."

Helen's reply echoed in the underpass beside the old school building that was Parkside Middle School.

The rain drizzled, dampening their clothes and frizzing their hair as they approached the roundabout in the town centre. The music was blasting.

"There it is." shouted Charlene above the noise, pointing her finger in the direction of the ride.

It was quite high and a bit like the Pirate Ship, but this one went all the way around. The Apollo had two cages, one either side of the big pivot, that held everything up.

As Charlene and Helen reached the ride they stood looking at the cages going in opposite directions and meeting at the top. The screams of excitement rang in their ears. They joined the queue.

"NEXT!" The man in the hut shouted.

They handed him their 80p and climbed up the steps, entering the cages. Charlene and Helen pulled down the safety bars over their heads and they sat in silence waiting for the attendant to secure their cage.

The engines started up and they both had butterflies in their stomachs. The ride began to move. They looked at each other, regretting ever stepping foot on the ride.

As they tipped upside down the yells from around seemed nothing compared to Helen's screaming.

"He-e-e-l-p!" was yelled so hard it nearly deafened her. They stopped in the air and when Helen looked down, all she could see was the green grass below her. She felt as though she was slipping out of the seat. Helen tried to convince herself that she was perfectly alright with the safety bar over her head and that she wasn't going anywhere. It was terrifying!

When it was over they got off the ride and Charlene had to sit down, her eyes were thumping. Helen couldn't walk straight! Her eyes were hurting and she need to sit down too.

After a few minutes, they got their bearings, stood up, and joined the queue to go on again.

Helen Scott Age 13

Brockwell Middle School Cramlington.

Repertory theatre returns to Blyth's Theatre Royal [*May 1950*]
A fire destroys the Theatre Royal bar causing damage estimated at £2,000. [*June 1950*]

Blyth Operatic Society marked the return of light opera to the town after an absence of twenty years with their production of 'Maid of the Mountains' [*April 1960*]

Dramatic Moments

It was a sad sight to see the demolition of the old Theatre Royal in Blyth behind the bus station. In its final years it became derelict warehouse; it deserved better. Arthur Jefferson, father of Stan Laurel (of Laurel and Hardy fame) was the manager of the theatre and had a strong association with Blyth. Jefferson Street, also pulled down, was named after him.

George Formby appeared on stage there and so did Tom Mix the film-star cowboy. I even heard that Ellen Terry, the famous Victorian classical actress played at the theatre.

'White Horse Inn' at the Theatre Royal, Blyth, 1961

In the 50's and 60's there was a popular professional repertory company based at the Theatre Royal and a leading lady from that time was Joan Francis who later joined Pat Phoenix in Coronation Street where she played Elsie Tanner's best friend. A young South African who started his acting career at Blyth was Alan Johns. Soon after, he changed his name to Stratford Johns and achieved national fame as Inspector Barlow of 'Z Cars' and 'Softly, Softly'.

In the early 1970's when I first came to live and work in the town, Blyth amateur dramatics seemed to going through a golden period. Brian Seddon and Julia Smith were wonderful in Arthur Miller's 'The Crucible', Trevor Harder was superb as Emcee in David Garrett's production of 'Cabaret' and Frank Scott was turning out a bravura performance as Professor Higgins in 'My Fair Lady' for the Blyth Operatic Society. Brian Lambert was the talented, enthusiastic Musical Director for the show and his recent death was a sad loss to the society and the town.

The Blyth Valley Players with Marie and Winnie Chicken at the helm were so impressive and ambitious that I decided to join them. It was here that I met Tom Easton; an old stager with a charismatic stage presence. Tom was an English teacher by day and an actor in the evenings. His colourful acting career began in local plays and he later 'trod the boards' of Blyth's Theatre Royal when the 'rep' company needed extra performers in the 1950's. Tom's wages went up in smoke:

"They gave me 40 Players cigarettes for a week's work and made me join Equity."

Mr Earl Armstrong introduces the new season for his repertory theatre company

Another well-known local actor, Jimmy Russell, would often perform with Tom. They were noted for their 'busking' on stage; in other words, not knowing their lines. They could improvise their way through a scene

but it was nerve-wracking playing alongside them if you were waiting for 'cues', as the dialogue often bore no relation to the script. Tom tells of an on-stage incident with Jimmy when his friend had no idea what his next line was. With great presence of mind, and still in character, he appealed to Tom saying:

"Tell me sir.. if you were in my position at this very moment.. what would you say to me?"

"Sir.." replied Tom, also in character, "I haven't the faintest idea."

Tom enjoyed a drink and when the Phoenix Theatre opened in Beaconsfield Street in Blyth it was handy venue for The Royal Tavern on the corner of the street. In one particular production Tom checked the script and worked out that in the second act there was a good 15 pages of the play (about 20 minutes) before he was due to appear again, so in costume and make-up he wandered off for a quick pint. Predictably, on stage, wrong lines were delivered and a huge chunk of dialogue - five pages of it - were lost. The prompt could see that Tom was due to make his entrance over the page and he wasn't in the building. Panic! Someone sprinted to the pub and Tom returned. I am told that without breaking his stride, he stepped off the street, into the theatre and directly onto the stage to deliver his lines. His timing was impeccable. As he exited, Tom continued the walk back to the pub to finish his beer.

Another Tom story, (probably apocryphal) told of a critical moment at the end of the first Act of an Agatha Christie thriller. A unknown corpse is found in the library and the police need to identify the body; the story hinges on the identification. Tom's character, Fenton, was the brother of the dead man and as the inspector pulled back the blanket he asked gravely:

"Is this your brother?"

Tom replied:

"Is it?"

And the curtain came down to end the first Act.

Tom should have said "It is!" He had remembered the words but had placed them in the wrong order; a simple enough mistake. The audience were left in confusion and apparently a front of house announcement confirmed that yes, the body in the library <u>was</u> the brother of Fenton. Behind the scene, the producer demanded an explanation.

"We've been rehearsing all week.." said Tom ".. I knew my part backwards!"

[Tom died on the 28th September 1996]

Andy Griffin

Blyth

ALL THE PEOPLE I MEET...

Friends And Relations

by the children of Eastlea First School, Cramlington

MY STEP-DAD

Every time Stephen walks in the sitting room
he is wearing things for the gym.
My mam and me, and my baby brother,
can easily make him laugh.
He's got big hands and he goes swimming
and weight-lifting.
He chucks me onto the settee
Or lifts me up to the ceiling so I can touch the lampshade.
On the wall he's put up spears and swords
And he's got a box-full of photos
and things from when he was in the army.
I love him a lot.
It's great when he gives my mam a shuggy.

Sarah Holman Age 8

UNCLE PETER

My Uncle Peter is a very happy, funny person
And he wears jeans all the time.
He has hairs all over his chest just like a gorilla.
He likes atlases and he's got maps on his walls.
For his holidays he goes all over the world to places like Holland, Mexico and Cumbria.
Uncle Peter loves a good meal and a good drink and he's got a Newcastle season ticket..
but he's still special to me.

Rachel Nicholson Age 8

GEMMA

My best friend is called Gemma.
Gemma's mam likes fashion
But Gemma doesn't.
She would rather wear jeans and stuff like that,
She looks awful in her long beige dress with white flowers on.
Gemma thinks she's ugly with freckles
But I don't, I think she looks OK.
I'm a bit sorry for Gemma because she is allergic to animals.
Her house is the same as mine
Apart from the dining room, kitchen and bedrooms.
She likes different things to me
And that's good because she has great ideas when we play.

Jennifer Sykes Age 8

AUNTIE JOAN

My Auntie Joan took me out to the Bay Horse
With Nana Peel and Nana Campbell.
I had pork, carrots, peas and chips
And a very, very, very big Yorkshire.
I ate it all up and Auntie gave me a pound and I said
"Thankyou"
She is very nice because she takes me to Whitley Bay
And sometimes as a special treat we go to Cullercoats beach.
I love it when Auntie Joan lets me help with her clothes parties.

Uncle John is in a wheelchair because he suddenly went weak.
He's got a sort of seat that goes up the bannister when you press a button.
I sometimes have a ride and it's good fun.

Jaimee Carr Age 8

Auntie Joan
and Uncle John
by Jaimee Carr

JOSHUA

Joshua is my little baby cousin and he's not yet one.
He wears a nice little baby-gro and he always has a smile on his face when you play with him.
He doesn't have any hobbies yet but he has lots of toys in his cot.
I once had a photograph taken with him and I had to hold his dodo in his mouth because he was crying and he kept spitting it out.
Little Joshua looks like my Uncle Alan, and he's six-foot-one!

Claire Louise Chambers
Age 8

Miss Nancy Barron was elected Coronation Year
Miss Blyth following a News Post poll. More than
1,000 people voted [*May 1953*]
Four year old Emma Mason of Matthew Road,
Blyth, hits the headlines as the new Miss Pears.
[*July 1981*]

RAG AND BONE MAN

A-car-a-har A-car-a-har

In muffler and cap
Old Handratty
Walks the street

Wooden cart spokes
Rumbling
Slowly turning

A-car-a-har A-car-a-har

Prams, pans,
Rusty bedsteads
Bicycle frames.
Woollens, worn shoes,
Mattresses

A-car-a-har A-car-a-har

Week in, week out.
From Ballast Hill
And back
Walking, calling.
Old Handratty
Ragged moustache
Ancient bones

A-car-a-har A-car-a-har

Brian Watson Cramlington

Blyth man, Mr Ernest McGarrigle of Newsham Road, who escaped from three different prison camps during the war before becoming an instructor for the French Resistance, received the Distinguished Conduct Medal from the King. [*May 1947*]
Gunner Joseph Hepple, a Korean POW, arrived home to Hartford Colliery. [*Sept. 1953*]

The Seaton Delaval Santa

Some of the most memorable days at Seaton Delaval were when Santa Claus arrived at the village by aeroplane to present an apple and an orange to every boy and girl.

The benefactor of this was Mr Alec Harper who owned a small shop at 78/80 Astley Road. He was helped by Mary, his devoted sister, and neither of them ever married. Alec and Mary were well liked in the village. He began his business in the mid 1920's and after a few years he had the idea of bringing Santa Claus to his shop the Saturday before Christmas.

Santa Claus's Plane in field – 1934

For the first year or two, Santa (a local character Jimmy Harbertson) came on the train. Father Christmas would board at Seghill station, complete with beard, red coat and bag of toys, and alight at Seaton Delaval station to be greeted by many children. He would lead a procession to Alec's shop where boxes and crates of fruit were laid out on the very wide pavement. Every child received an apple and an orange - free!

After 1930 Alec engaged an aeroplane to bring Santa. It was more exciting watching the aircraft appear in the sky and then land in the field. The plane, a De Havilland Moth, G-AALG was piloted by Captain Irving of the Newcastle Aero Club who gave his services free. He flew from Cramlington airfield (now non-existent) and landed in a field opposite Foreman's Row (now demolished). A crowd of youngsters, much enlarged by children from the surrounding villages, gathered around the plane. From the field they all followed Santa down to the shop to receive their fruit.

A brass band, complete with banner, would lead the parade and one year, Uncle Nick of the Evening Chronicle Gloops Club came to join in the fun. Uncle Nick and his white cat, Gloops (someone dressed up) were very well-known and there were plenty of young members (known as gloopers) in the crowds that day but Gloops did not come to Seaton Delaval on this occasion.

The event became so well known that for two years the Pathe Gazette, a film company which produced newsreels for the cinema, brought their cameras here to record the proceedings in 1934 and 1935. Mr Harper received copies of film and I later showed them on my 35mm projector which I had actually bought at Harper's shop many years earlier. The films delighted many middle-aged residents who were seeing themselves as youngsters. The war stopped the visits to the village and Santa never arrived again by aeroplane.

The walk to the shop. Alec Harper (lfront left with the bear) Uncle Nick with bow tie 1935

Mary Harper 1959   Tom Allan Collection

Alec Harper's sister Mary died in 1964 and the following year he installed a clock on the frontage of the Council Offices in Avenue Road. The clock strikes every hour and it is regarded by many old timers in the village as 'Mary's clock'. Mr Alec Harper died in 1968 and both are buried in Seghill Churchyard.

Tom 'Tot' Allan Seaton Delaval

Meggie [1950]

We had a neighbour called Meggie. She was known as the silent visitor. Meggie was a stout lady who always wore carpet slippers during her frequent calls to people's homes. We would be taken by surprise as her large figure would suddenly appear out the back, or there would an unexpected knocking on the living room door; no-one heard her coming. Meggie never sat down on her visits and she would carry on a conversation as though detached from the ownership of her eyes; they had a separate interest of their own by gazing around the room and taking everything in. Meggie spoke in a low voice that was devoid of expression and seemed to lack a beginning or end. She had been a fish-gutter on the River Blyth when the fishing fleets used to come in but like many women in the neighbourhood she took in washing for half-a-crown [12$\frac{1}{2}$p] a week.

Meggie's brother, Johnny, was a quietly spoken man who worked at Crofton Mill Pit. Unlike his sister who he shared the house with, you could always hear him coming. The clatter from his approaching studded pit boots could be heard from a long way off as he returned home from work. His smooth skin would be coal-black beneath the helmet but his face always wore the same placid expression. Johnny was a craftsman in his spare time. He had a treadle lathe in a hut at the bottom of the garden and he took orders for lamp standards, candlesticks, cigarette stands and table lamps - anything that could be turned in wood. The finished articles, varnished so the grain stood out, were distinctive and much sought after. However, if light switches or wires were needed, you had to do that yourself because Johnny was afraid of anything to do with electricity.

Brian Watson Cramlington

DAY CENTRE

Sitting in our circle of seats
We throw a ball at each other.
'Good for wheelchair posture' we're told

But what does it do for the brain?

We used to have quizzes
And stimulating conversations.

I'm not one for dominoes
Or colouring in with felt-tip pens.

I could make a plastic tea-pot stand
But who would thank me for it?

Truth is...
I don't want to play ball.

Scotch Fisher Girls, Blyth

Marjorie Hooks Seaton Delaval

Mr Edward Milne, a 45 year old Scottish trade union official, was elected Member of Parliament for the Blyth constituency with a majority of 16,163. [*November 1960*]
Eddie Milne was expelled from the Labour Party but decided to go it alone as an independent and was returned as Blyth's MP by more than 6,000 votes. [*March 1974*]

A victory for London barrister John Ryman in the General Election. Eddie Milne, who lost by 78 votes considers calling for a 'replay'.
[*October 1974*]
Following John Ryman's decision to stand down as MP for Blyth, Ronnie Campbell wins the seat for Labour. [*June 1987*]

Ernie

At the end of the war there were many casualties that were not the result of injury. Countless refugees lost their homes and family and could not return. My husband John met Ernie, one of those 'displaced persons', in a Blyth pub. He was a highly skilled sea-going joiner from Latvia and he lived aboard ship. By the late 1940's Russia had a stranglehold over the Eastern European countries and they picked up the pieces of war-torn Hungary and Poland. The Iron Curtain came down and Ernie was cut off from his wife and two children. He was never to see them again.

John made friends with Ernie who admitted there was 'nothing but the bottle' in his life. When Ernie was brought to meet us he asked:

"Can this be my harm?"

In his broken English we knew he meant 'home'. His words were heartbreaking. Ernie became a member of the family and was much-loved by the children. He stayed with us in Blyth whenever he was in port and was respectful and courteous but still had a wonderful sense of fun. The Reid family remember Ernie at the dinner table pointing dolefully at his plate saying:

"Thankyou.. but I am no a friend to the carrot.".

It distressed Ernie that he no longer had roots so I made him a collection of our family photographs and he cherished that album. He called John his brother, and me his sister. Ernie had no past to get in touch with. It was bad enough that he had no future.. but no past? He was a lost soul; a victim of war in peacetime.

One December, when Ernie was away at sea, we received a large box almost as tall as me and three feet wide [1m]. In it, there were two perfect Christmas trees with a hand-carved wooden stand, from Ernie. He and his bosun had put their jobs at risk by leaving the ship in the Arctic Circle to cut down and send, a special gift to his Blyth family. I wrote immediately because we were so touched but he never received the letter.

Ernie later married a Blyth woman and the last time he called was when John died at the early age of 52. He sat by the kitchen range and wept. The loss of his 'brother' was very real. "I have my memories" were has last words to me.

The real tragedy is that he did not live to see the dismantling of the Berlin Wall and the new-found freedom of the Baltic States. Latvia and Lithuania are welcoming the return of their displaced people but for Ernie it came too late.

Jean Reid Blyth

Seaton Delaval couple, Ivan and Anne Marie Windsor, gave birth to their second set of twin girls in 18 months. [*August 1986*]

Diabetic nurse, Ann Trewick of Blyth, made British medical history at Newcastle Freeman Hospital when she became the first person to have an insulin pump inserted. [*March 1984*]

Chernobyl Children

In March 1991, Michael and I read an article in the national newspaper asking if any families in England would be willing to give children from Chernobyl a holiday, to enable them to breathe fresh air, eat fresh food and play on uncontaminated soil. I was surprised to learn that by staying in our country for just one month, 43% of the radiation in the child's body is eradicated. We wrote straight away.

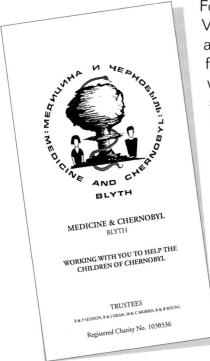

Four months later we received an unexpected phone call from Vadim Bukat of Minsk - he was ringing us from Seaton Delaval! He asked if we could take five children. Could we place them with families in the Blyth area? I said "Yes." immediately. I had no idea what I was taking on. I talked with friends and there was no shortage of volunteer families. The official forms asked what sex we would prefer and curiously we all said 'girls'.

We heard no more for a while, then unexpectedly I received word that the party would be landing at Manchester airport - in seven days time! I panicked, but my friend Joy Gillespie came to the rescue and her father, through the Rotary Club, arranged for us to borrow Tynedale High School's mini bus. Brian and Pauline Seddon drove us to Manchester where we were due to meet the 10:30am flight. Back in Newsham I had laid on a huge spread for their arrival. Unfortunately, due to snow in Moscow, the flight was eight and a half hours late and when we finally met up with our visitors, we saw five very tired and frightened young boys with Dr Igor Kot, their interpreter. Andre, Danny, Ivan, Alexander and Sacha, who were from a Chernobyl orphanage, had spent the past two days travelling and there was another mini-bus journey of over 100 miles awaiting them. We delivered them to their host families in the early hours of the morning; not the welcome we had intended.

Although the children spoke no English and we had only phrase-book Russian, the next four weeks were great. We took them on outings and the local shops donated clothes and toys. They had a wonderful time - and so did the families! The four weeks went over very quickly and it was an emotional scene at Gallowgate as we said our good-byes. We never expected to see the boys again.

Afterwards we all agreed that the visit should not be a 'one-off', so we made enquiries and learnt that if we could pay the fares and finance the trip, then the children could return. We immediately set about raising the money by forming a committee and eventually registered as a charity; Medicine & Chernobyl, Blyth. The people in the Borough were very generous and this was brought home in January 1992 when we heard that the orphanages were short of food and that the children were starving. Ferguson's Transport of Blyth stepped in and provided a large lorry plus Colin Lilburn, the driver. We filled the vehicle with £30,000-worth of food, clothing and medical supplies. Two of our committee made the journey to make sure the gifts reached their proper destination.

That same year we brought fourteen children over, including our original five. Each year since, we have increased our numbers and this summer we managed thirty in Blyth, twenty in Gateshead and five in Cumbria. My ambition is to bring all 250 children from the orphanage for a month's holiday every year. I fill out the lottery each week, you never know.

The visits really benefit the children. In their own towns they are sickly and suffer from nose-bleeds. The radiation has made the youngsters impotent which effectively means a whole generation has been wiped out. Babies born since the 1986 nuclear power station leak have suffered deformities and terminal illness. Apart from the care these children receive in our community, there is no doubt that their physical condition improves too.

I often get asked how we can communicate with children who cannot speak our language. It's easy. You smile, you cuddle, you love and reassure them - just like any child. In return you receive affection and appreciation. Love is a universal language isn't it? Since responding to that item in the newspaper I have had six years of many rewarding experiences that I wouldn't have missed for the world.

Christine Morris Newsham

From Dr Kot

October 1991

Dear Friends

We Bielorussian Chernobyl children are extremely thankful for your attention, help and care you are giving us.

We'll take home in our hearts a grateful remembrance of your really wonderful people. You've contributed to make our stay in Blyth happy and unforgettable.

With love and gratitude.

Thankfully yours.

[signed by all the children]

Blyth Rotary Club named Christine Morris as 'Citizen of the Year' for her work in setting up the Children of Chernobyl Appeal. [*June 1992*]

Pillar Of The Church [1930]

There was some characters then. I well remember Mr Burns, he was a pillar of St John's Church. He would stand by the door on Sundays and if he didn't like your face you didn't get in. He was a real puritan and he would clip a lad around the head if he heard them using bad language. He worked on Loco 12 at the colliery and I remember him working there when I had just started at the pit. On this particular day the loco had come off the rails and this was at a time when the driver and firemen had to be responsible for their own engines. Well they couldn't shift it and you should have heard that man swear. I've never heard anything like it before or since.

Arthur Heayns Klondyke

Emma Nicholson, the daughter of a former Morpeth MP, is chosen as the prospective Conservative Party candidate for the Blyth constituency at the next General Election. [*May 1976*]

Margaret Thatcher visits Cramlington on her first tour of the North East as Prime Minister. [*May 1980*]

From A Blyth Nursery

GRANDMA
by Clare

My Grandma comes to my house.
She's got grey hair and she looks old.
My Grandma wears a dress with different colours.
She goes to Spain and she sits down on a towel.

GRANDMA
by Marie

My Grandma is special to me and my Grandad is too.
My Grandma wears gold glasses and she has got a posh house like Hyacinth.
She has got the flu now.

UNCLE NORMAN
by Graham

My Uncle Norman is funny.
He wears a Newcastle strip and he likes bird watching.
He's seen a dodo at the Hancock Museum.

MY DAD
by Gavin

My Dad has got brown hair.
I think he is strong.
He wears jeans and t-shirts.
When he is hot he takes his Rainbow t-shirt off.
He lifts me up and makes me laugh because he says he is going to drop me.

ON THE SUBJECT OF THE MAYOR'S PROPOSED NEW DAIMLER
[To the Blyth News (1976)]

Wor Mayor's a canny sort of chap
An' when he walks I'll doff me cap
But if he's bought this limousine
He wants a brick through winderscreen.
TWENTY THOUSAND! Too much by far
To spend wor cash on a civic car.
Nee doot it's gorra sunshine roof
All armour plate and bullet-proof
It'll have to be, or like as not,
Someone's sure to have him shot!
Colour telly, Super Car,
Built-in netty, cocktail bar,
With Broon on draught and ice-cool 'Fed'
And back seats like a double bed.
Nee wonder Treasurer's looking chuffed;
They ought to have him burned and stuffed!

If you should print this little letter
Perhaps he'll spend wor money better.

Bill Bennett, Bebside.

For the first time in the Borough of Blyth's history, all the civic heads will be female. The new mayor-elect, Councillor Jean Tate, chose her daughter Mrs Josephine Kulke as her Mayoress and Mrs Vivienne Crosby was elected as Deputy Mayor. [*May 1978*]

Seaton Delaval Cycling Club – 1934

Tom Allan Collection

The Duke of Edinburgh pays a flying visit to Wellesley Nautical School landing in a helicopter on the school playing field. [*June 1960*]

Sir John Hunt, leader of the successful Everest expedition, made a flying visit to the Wellesley Nautical School where he was presented with a shepherd's crook [*Feb 1961*]

Dad [Extract]

The first man I remember in my life was Dad. He was a big strong noisy man; rather like a bulldozer, giving the feeling of clearing all before him. Dad laughed often and very loudly but his sense of humour was sometimes rather misplaced and he was guilty of finding great amusement in other people's downfall. This brought a quiet word of disapproval from my more gentle Mam. There was no way a deaf person would have any difficulty hearing the spoken word from this big man. When wanting to emphasise anything he was saying, Dad would point the index finger of his right hand into the air. This fascinated me because the second knuckle of this finger was permanently bent, having been injured some time before. It always held my attention; it had such authority.

When tea was over, table cleared, dishes washed and put away, the family would settle down with their various hobbies. On cold winter nights as the wind hammered at the doors and windows in an effort to intrude and the gaslights spluttered and waved about, the room felt cosy and safe. Mam's steel knitting needles made a tinny clicking noise as she knit yet another pair of socks. My older brother sat on the floor building up weird and wonderful creations with his Meccano set. Before settling down for the evening, Dad would put a chock of wood on the fire, covering it with coals for continued warmth. It sat there giving up the ghost to an accompaniment of spits and cracks with orange sparks darting about like rocketed fireflies. Through the fireguard I would gaze at the castles and caves which appeared as the fire burned up and I would look for 'fire fairies'. Dad had two mouth organs and he often sat playing one in the evening before I was packed off to bed. I liked the smaller of the two although I must admit that the tunes were not so good played on this. It was a tiny thing; the velvet-lined box it lived in was only about one-and-a-half inches long [4cm].

On summer evenings after tea, Dad would read the paper and listen to the news on the radio (no-one dare speak when the news was on) then he would go outside to be busy. Chocks of wood were brought to the back door and Dad would sit on the step with his chopping axe. I would play with my dolls nearby and listen to the dull thug, thug, as he began to chop, then came the splitting sound as the axe parted the wood and finally the metallic chink as the axe hit the cement beneath. He kept a big box inside the cupboard at the side of the fireplace filled with these resin-scented sticks. My toys were kept on the shelf above the box and I loved to open the door and smell the wood.

Dorothy Redpath Blyth

Pamela Watson of Marine Terrace, Blyth, proved she was the world's fastest knitter by producing a sweater in under three hours for presenter Jayne Irving during TV AM's live challenge. [*March 1985*]

An ex-Blyth man, who went on to win the Military Cross, Col Henry 'Sweeney' Todd, was the subject of Eamon Andrew's 'This is Your Life'. His three sisters who still live in the area, featured on the programme. [*March 1985*]

JACKIE'S GONG

[Jack Allen was a well-known and respected Youth Leader for 38 years at the Blyth Boy's Club. His dedicated service to the young people of the town was recognised on his retirement; he was awarded the British Empire Medal in the New Year's Honours List.]

Wor Jackie's got a medal
He's gannin' to London Toon
To meet Hor Gracious Majesty
He's tekkin' his marras doon.

He's got speshial dispensation
To tek an extra day
It'll be another halliday
Withoot a cut in pay.

He's rigged oot in a Dobson hat
An' elastic-sided boots
Fancy socks and doe-skin gloves
To gan with 'ees claa-hamma suit.

5 a-side football at the Blyth Sports Centre

Hor Majesty will have great pleashor
An' aal the bills she'll pay
An' order Gilbert Barker
To grant Blyth a halliday.

She'll meet Jack at the station
She'll drive him roond the Strand
To the tune of Blaydon Races
By the Cowpen Colliery Band.

Wor Jack's got other medals
For fighting in the past -
Dodgin' German submarines
Nine years 'before the mast'.

He's got six for playin' snooker
And two for playin' darts
An' one for suppin' yards of ale
An' a gowld for martial arts.

So where he'll put the other one?
Remains a guess to most
But when they hear him walkin'
He'll soond like Marley's Ghost.

Bill Bennett Bebside

A row blew up among youth leaders and parents after M E Davies, general secretary of Blyth YMCA invited 'hippies' to attend the centre. [*September 1967*]

Newcastle United star Jimmy 'Jinky' Smith marries Helen Forster in Cramlington [*October 1975*]

IN THE JUVENILE COURT

[Jack Hart of Blyth, a retired policeman, recalls an affection he felt for George, a wayward 14 year old, who he was duty bound to arrest and charge with petty theft]

Jekyll and Hydes are we,
George, the Magistrate and me:
George as he stands and answers
in his voice in which timid defiance rings
that tears the soul
- dressed in top coat
over nothing at all,
trousers short and shoes misshapen,
I suspect too large,
and overall, invisible,
a cloak of steel.

As I stand, I look at him
and he at me.
I feel like a traitor of the first degree
as I prove Charges One, Two and Three,
for I have pierced the cloak
and seen eyes laughing
for an instant
and I know there is hope
for him, if not for me.

The Magistrate sits and ponders
the rules set out by the learned clerk.
He pushes and pulls with all his might
mixing expedient mercy
with what is right.
In the end, he raises his eyes
and says dully,
'You are remanded in custody for one week',
and we, George, the magistrate and me,
sigh wearily.

Jack Hart Blyth

Two Blyth fishermen Reginald Jacobs (Newsham) and Thomas Wilkinson (Cowpen) spent 40 hours in a life-raft after their boat sank; they were eventually picked up by a Russian ship. [*December 1972*]

Blyth art-lover, Peter Neave, returned home after being thrown into a Paris jail for trying to steal a Van Gogh painting. [*March 1973*]
A car maintenance class at Blyth attracted over 100 applicants. [*January 1953*]

THERE ARE PLACES I REMEMBER...

A Place In The Heart

I have supported Newcastle United since I saw my first game in 1930. During that time I have seen great footballers but I have no difficulty in selecting my favourite player. Not surprisingly, because I come from Ashington, it was Jackie Milburn. I am proud to be able to say that I saw every game that he played in at St James' Park as well as the three FA Cup Finals at Wembley where Jackie played such an important part.

The day after Jackie died Radio Newcastle repeated a broadcast he had made a year earlier. The programme was called 'A Place in the Heart'. I taped the interview and this is now one of my precious treasures which brings back happy memories of a truly great sportsman. One interesting section is when Jackie was talking about Seaton Sluice. I recall, verbatim, what he said:

"I was talking to a chap one day about football. I asked him where he lived. He said 'Seaton Sluice'. I said 'There's not much there is there?' He said 'Don't you believe it, Jackie. We've got the best of both worlds. In the space of one hundred yards we have the seaside and back over behind the bridge we've got the dene and you're completely in the country.' When I heard this I started to laugh.

At that time my daughter lived in Seaton Sluice. She gave birth to my first grandchild. There is nothing finer in the world than seeing your children's children. I couldn't keep away from Seaton Sluice. I used to take my granddaughter for walks (Laura we called her, after my wife) and it hit me what that fellow had said. We went to the sea front then I used to vary it and go down the back. I got the shock of my life. It was completely true what the man had said. The country and the seaside all belong to Seaton Sluice. I spent hours there, just Laura and I. This went on for three glorious years."

George Davison Ashington

Home Sweet Home

Don't ask me why, but every time we've been out anywhere, as soon as we pass Nelson Hill, I know that we are home. It doesn't matter whether we have been away for a day, a week, or even an afternoon, I always associate Nelson Hill with home.

I don't know why because I have never been up it, I've never even stood near it. Some people see Nelson Hill as a great big mound of earth with a bit of grass on top, but it is more than that. It tells a story of past and present and to me it symbolises home.

You see, years ago, when Cramlington was still a mining town, the hill was just another slag heap. That was, until somebody decided to grass it over and turn it into a proper hill. Now it is a popular play area for children and during the winter months it provides the perfect place for sledging.

So, things are not always as they seem at first glance. To you, it might just look like another hill but to me it represents the warmth and security which I associate with being home sweet home.

Gemma Davis Age 13

Brockwell Middle School, Cramlington

Sledging Down Nelson Hill

I remember a few years ago now, it was winter and it was stotting down with snow. I got wrapped up in my warmest clothes. Me, my sister and our neighbours grabbed our sledges and headed towards Nelson Hill.

My sister pulled me all the way and we walked past happy people throwing snowballs. There must have been a hundred snowmen. I'll never forget approaching the hill and feeling small as an ant. We scrambled all the way and when we finally reached the top my sister and I climbed into our yellow plastic sledge. I remember feeling a rush of excitement flutter through my body.

One, two, three.. we flew down the hill like swallows taking flight. The wind blew through my hair but the next thing I knew we were both lying at the bottom of the hill, covered in snow. We got up laughing and headed back to the top of the hill.

Nicola Cooper (Age 13)

... we could see Nelson Hill covered in snow and as we got nearer the distant excitement and delight grew louder. Helen and I stood at the foot of a giant ice-cream that was dotted with hundreds and thousands. We slowly started to climb.

Eventually we reached the peak and looked down on the whole town. A white sheet of snow covered the area from the cold North Sea to the Cheviot Hills way out in the distance.

We set our sledges on the slope, clambered on, and pushed ourselves away.

Hayley Blair (Age 12)

... within a split-second we were three-quarters of the way down and it was then I fell off the back of my neighbour's sledge. I rolled down and down to the bottom of the hill. My dad and sister were right behind and their sledge flew over my head. I felt the force of my dad's boot in my face. They quickly stopped and my dad was apologetic and horrified at what had happened. A patch of snow beneath me had turned red from the blood pouring out of my nose. I overheard a big lad say:

"Wow! Did you see that? It must have knacked!"

When I heard this, I smiled and felt good. That lad must have thought I was dead hard.

Michael Sean O'Neill (Age 13)

Pupils of Brockwell Middle School, Cramlington

In The Air [Extract from Kramel Kid]

At Nelson Village there was an airship shed and facilities for making dirigible air-craft. I believe only one was produced and that was an advertising balloon which read: 'WALTER WILLSON ON TOP'. One day it was flying around and so too was a black De Havilland Moth bi-plane. The aeroplane made a forced landing in a field at Shankhouse. I raced off on my cycle to get a closer look but I got a puncture. I ended up walking home pushing my bike behind the D H Moth. It's wings were folded and it was being towed to Cramlington aerodrome which was situated to the west of where Bassington Trading Estate stands now. One of the pilots was the son of Lord Runciman, the ship owner.

He wasn't the only personality to appear at the aerodrome. Thousands of people would flock there to see the air shows which included a flying circus, aerobatic displays and RAF planes showing off their skills. The famous 'King's Cup Air Race' included Cramlington Aerodrome as one of its refuelling stops. I saw Kingsford Smith, Jim Mollison and the famous pilot who was later to be his wife, Amy Johnson. There were always long queues for a trip round the area which cost five shillings. The parachute drop was a very big attraction. In the 1930's it was a dangerous and precarious activity.

Leslie Miners Cramlington

Amy Johnson's Aircraft 'Jason' at Cramlington Airfield

Newcastle United footballers, who were beaten by Manchester City in the League Cup Final, were given a tremendous welcome by employees of Wilkinson Sword, Cramlington when they visited the factory. [*February 1976*]

Workers at Burberry's factory at Kitty Brewster, Blyth, celebrate after winning the Queen's Award for industry for the 5th time. [*September 1986*]

The China Hill (Northburn)

Years ago, the park near my home wasn't there. Instead, all that stood was mound of earth, a mountain of soil the size of a house. But there was something special about it.

Many a bleak Saturday, I would get on my bike and go to China Hill, armed with a plastic bag. I would climb to the peak and search for broken bits of china.

There was tons of it; white, red, black, blue, large, small. All shone brightly in the mid-day sun.

Once my bag was fairly full, I clambered back on my bike and cycled home again. Then, I would look at my findings and sort them out into piles of the same colours. I once found four pieces which made half a saucer.

But the council were soon informed of Cramlington's young kids who were having to make up games and going to muddy hills to play. They decided to erect a park and they situated it right on the top of China Hill.

Now I am older I realise that the park is probably a much safer and better idea. The China Hill is now lost for ever - but not in my memory.

Mark Rutherford Age 12

Brockwell Middle School, Cramlington

Blyth Power Station is linked to the National Grid and begins operations after 3½ years in construction. [*December 1958*]
The fourth and last chimney at Blyth Power Station reached its ultimate height of 552 feet [180 meters] [*August 1963*]

Workmen busy on construction of a 275,000 volt line from Cambois power station to Yorkshire, narrowly escaped injury when scaffolding 150 yards long and 40 ft high collapsed in a gale near Seaton Delaval. [*May 1961*]

Blyth Power Station 1962

The Long Grass

I have played in the Long Grass since I was really small. It is a big open space with trees and long thin wispy grass.

It is next to my house between Brockwell Middle School and Burnside School in Cramlington and my friends Laura Hodgen and Gemma Barber have always played there with me.

In winter, just before the sun goes down, the trees are spooky and if your imagination takes control, they look at you and seem to be laughing.

In the summer we run through the lush green grass and in the winter we play in the thick deep snow.

When we were small we played detectives. One was the murderer and the other two had to chase them. It was great fun.

Sadly, even though we have sent letters and a petition, in a couple of years, the builders will be coming to destroy the Long Grass.

Becky Beeby (Age 11)

St Peter's Middle School, Cramlington

A familiar Malvin's Close landmark disappears as the 75 foot [23m] water tower at Bates Colliery is blown up by demolition experts [*March 1961*]

Plessey Woods

Plessey Woods is full of opportunities to relax and have fun.

There are many different walks to take and there is a river to play in. We go there to have picnics in the summer and in the autumn we go there for walks to see the beautiful golden brown leaves.

Sometimes me and my best friend, Becky, ride to Plessey Woods on our bikes. We leave the bikes at the shop and go and make great big piles of leaves. Becky and I jump on them and we fall over, laughing.

We also make dens in the trees and stay there all day until it's time to go home.

Soon a part of this area will be destroyed by open cast mining. It is a controversial issue and conferences, debates and demonstrations have taken place about this matter.

It would be very sad if this area's beauty was to be lost forever.

Kate Burdis (Age 11)

St Peter's Middle School, Cramlington

The 'Chiviots'

My paternal grandparents lived in one of a row of very old stone houses. These were on a cobbled road sloping down towards the quayside. As a very small child I used to be taken by my older brother on an occasional 'duty visit'. Sometimes Grandad would take us down to see the fishing boats at the riverside. He knew all the fishermen by name - I was really impressed by this. I would watch the men mending their nets as they joked and talked. Each one of them seemed to be holding a little clay pipe clenched between his teeth. The memory of the smell of tobacco, freshly caught fish and the salty sea has stayed with me throughout my life.

I would see the cargo ships slowly making their way along the river, dark smoke billowing from their funnels, hooters sounding, warning everyone of their approach. Some flat-decked ships carried timber, whilst the colliers were loaded with coal from the local mines. Dad used to tell me these were known as 'black diamonds'. Pilot boats and tugs were such busy little vessels going about their daily business. Sometimes I would see an elegant yacht threading her way through the bigger traffic, her gleaming white sails bringing relief to the sombre scene. Always there was the screaming and wheeling of gulls and the thwack! thwack! of the dark water hitting the wall at the side of the quay.

On a clear day, Grandad, a man of few words, bent down to my level and pointed along and beyond the river. In the distance I could see hills. "Them's the Chiviots" he said. At my tender age the 'Chiviots' didn't mean a thing, but since Grandad rarely spoke, I knew these words were important. I never forgot that day. It was nothing spectacular, but it seemed to lie dormant in the back of my mind.

Quite a few years passed, and my Mum and I went on a bus with other mothers and children to visit my brother Tom, when he was at a Boy's Brigade camp. Tom and his friend took me for a walk up the heather-covered hills. Everywhere was purple and there was so much space. I was overawed.

"These are the hills Grandad talked about" he told me.

I couldn't believe it. Were they so far away from Blyth? Further on, Tom found a stream and we stopped. The boys showed me how clear it was. I could see hundreds of smooth pebbles through the sparkling water. Tom took a chipped white enamel mug from his haversack and scooped up some water for me to drink. Never before, or since, has any water tasted so good. It was icy cold and so refreshing.

I was thinking about the walk and the exciting day we'd had as the bus rattled and bumped its way back to Blyth. I felt sleepy but my head was still full of the smell of the hillside, the heather and of course that mug of water.

"Mam, you know where we've been?" I said to her.

She smiled and nodded. "Yes pet, those were the Cheviots."

I was nearly asleep but I still had to have the last word.

"No, them's the Chiviots.. Grandad says."

Dorothy Redpath Blyth.

Oil lamps in the Norman Church of our Lady, next to Delaval Hall, are to be replaced by the latest type of concealed flourescent lighting. [*May 1957*]

The Mausoleum [A Short Story]

Tom Allan Collection

THE MAUSOLEUM, DELAVAL HALL. 1657

The Mausoleum, Seaton Delaval. Built 1776

The argument began in the morning.

"You are not! I've never heard of such a thing."

Ben's Mam stood with her feet astride, arms folded.

The twelve-year-old smiled lovingly at his Mam's defiant stance. He knew she wouldn't stay angry for long.

"But it's in the Wizard.. Wilson of the Wizard.. he lives in a barrel and has smashing adventures."

"You are not camping out in a rain barrel."

"But Mam" Ben pleaded "It's OK, it's in the Wizard."

His voice trailed away as his mother took refuge in a familiar phrase:

"We'll see what your father says about it."

Ben knew he could cajole his Mam but bitter experience told him his Dad's word was Law.

Later that evening when Ben was out his Mam and Dad laughed at their son's unusual request. They recalled how Ben had copied a character called Spiderman out of the Hotspur and how they had fetched the ladder to bring him down off the roof.

"That laddie has quite an imagination."

Mr Short thought about it.

"I can't see how he can do any harm with the old barrel. It's out the back so we can keep and eye on him."

Ben and his best friend Hylton Miller carefully lowered the large oaken barrel sideways then steadied it with balks of timber. They put two old clippy mats on the 'floor' then added a home-made clay lamp and a small picture. They used a sheet to cover the opening and with the candle lit there was a sense of cosiness and security from within.

"It's great, far better than any tent."

Ben thanked his Mam as she handed them tea and sandwiches.

She shivered in the cold and dark and let them know how she felt.

"You must be mad!"

But the boys were wild with excitement as they shouted their goodnights.

The next few days were spent in chatting and planning adventures. Mam grumbled as the boys kept her busy asking for tea and food. Dad laughed at his wife's complaints.

"They'll soon get tired of it. It can't be comfortable and anyway there's a storm due."

In fact the barrel was getting cold and the dampness and yowling cats kept them awake at night. Sleep was practically impossible as they twisted and turned on the sloping sides.

"Wilson was always having adventures but we haven't had one since we camped out."

Hylton, easing his body, echoed what Ben himself was thinking. Trouble was, the lads had a problem. They had boasted at school that they were living in a barrel and many youngsters were envious. The news soon spread and they basked in the fame and glory. At this moment they were cold and fed up but to save face they knew they had to stick it out.

Tom Allan Collection

Harby Hook – 1932

PC Joe Fryer was chatting to Mr Short at the Avenue Head but Ben was only half-listening to their conversation. His attention was held by Harvey Hook, the Salvation Army stalwart who sang and played his accordion. This small-ginger haired man regularly sang the praises of God through the well-loved hymns: Rock of Ages, The Old Rugged Cross, What a Friend we have in Jesus. His powerful voice was loved by the villagers. Even Joe Fryer hummed along. He had been the village bobby for years and most crime involved the local kids pinching apples or turnips; very few people had anything worth stealing and doors were rarely locked. Ben saw PC Fryer nudge his Dad and they both smiled at the appearance of another local character. Everyone in the village knew him, it was Bob the Tramp. Bob Hills described himself as a 'knight of the road' and with his long thick beard and straggling grey hair he was instantly recognisable. Seaton Delaval was his 'begging' area and with his humour and ready wit he was usually guaranteed a free drink or two at his local, The Delaval Arms. From across the road he gave the law-enforcer a grand wave.

"There's been a report of a savage dog roaming the village..."

PC Fryer was speaking and now Ben was listening.

"..it was seen snarling and growling and foaming at the mouth. Quite a size by all accounts. Last seen running down the Avenue towards the Hall. I've had a look round but seen nothing."

This was it. This was what they had waited for. Ben and Hylton knew all about mad dogs. Hadn't they stood transfixed outside the Queen's Hall Cinema and stared at the billboards advertising the horror film 'The Wolfman'? They knew all about Dracula and beasts with gleaming eyes and baring teeth? The mad dog of Delaval became a vicious, murderous werewolf in their imaginations. Their spirits were lifted, at last, an adventure.

Crouched in the barrel, the boys made plans to hunt down this wild creature and save the village. Preparations were feverish; two wooden crosses, wooden stakes (tent pegs) a bunch of onions (they couldn't get garlic) a hammer and a silver fork, it had to be silver. They knew these utensils would give them some form of protection, but as they waited for dusk, they had no idea how to use these deadly instruments.

Their time came. At first they ran eagerly down the wooded avenue and over the stubbled fields towards the Hall. The woods and the grazing cattle took on a sombre and menacing form. They knew this area well by daylight but in the darkness it awakened inner fears. It was a wild night, the wind moaned causing leafy branches to sway and rustle. Clouds scudded across the moonlit sky; a light and dark cameo. They paused, hearts pounding at the hoot of an owl. Hylton's voice trembled as he croaked.

"Mebbes we should go back."

Ben was determined.

"We'll push on, it's not far now."

They lifted their crosses a little higher, draped the onions around their neck, and ploughed on.

Eventually they reached their destination and stood at the moat overlooking the ruined mausoleum. The building had been erected two hundred years ago by the Delaval family to house the last remaining heir of the notorious dynasty. The local legends and oft repeated tales of the family gave an aura of dread. The mausoleum was said to be connected by tunnel to the nearby Seaton Delaval Hall so if there was a creature of the night this had to be its lair. The boys paused and listened. Was that the screech of a snared rabbit? Or was it the wind, whining and soughing? The atmosphere was nightmarish.

Derelict Dome 1987

Ben clambered over the cluttered debris that barred the doorway. He felt sure there were hidden eyes staring, daring them to proceed. Senses tense, looking to left and right. Hylton whispered.

"Light the candle."

In the dim glow they inched their way forward.

"Lift up the crosses."

Hylton obeyed Ben's trembling command. His mind was full of snarling beasts with bloody fangs. He clutched at his friend for comfort. Ben's heart lurched as he felt the hands upon him and he gave a smothered gasp through clenched teeth. Their fear was now tangible. There was a presence. An unknown terror was watching, waiting, and lying unseen in this burial chamber. An evil in the darkness.

It was Hylton who felt a soft, moving sensation under his feet. Ben saw the shadow of the two crosses illuminated by the light, then all Hell broke loose.

At first there was a terrified moaning, then a scream rose up from beneath them. Sheer horror anchored the boys as flailing limbs beat against their bodies. Before dropping the candle from his grasp Ben looked into the face of the werewolf. He saw its hairy bestial face and watched terror-stricken as its jaws opened and a blood-curdling howl was released. Now they moved. Their yells were answered by the chilling cries of the beast. Stakes, hammer, fork and onions were scattered as the friends fled from the howling behind them.

Hylton fell into the moat and lay there moaning. Ben came quickly to his senses. He had not been bitten or eaten, he was still alive. He gathered up his courage and found Hylton in a pitiable state. He was crying and near-hysterical yet still he held up his cross. Ben grabbed his friend and ran out of the woods shouting the Lord's Prayer. The boys ran as they had never run before. Not to the barrel, but home.. to a safe, secure, and strong home.

Mam was concerned. For the past two days Ben had not been his usual cheery self. She had heard that Hylton had not been to school and wondered if there had been a falling out, but Ben wasn't saying. Later that evening Ben's Dad came home with a small shivering terrier.

"There you are. Mebbes this'll cheer you up."

Dad presented the dog to Ben. His eyes lit up.

"Where did it come from?"

"A present from PC Fryer. This is the mad dog that's been terrifying the village. They were going to put it to sleep."

The dog gave a little whine. Ben put his arms around it.

"Can we keep it Dad?"

"You'll have to ask your Mam."

Ben's Mam was standing with a dish cloth in her hands and she was shaking her head; but she was smiling too. She went into the kitchen to get some bits and the dog started licking Ben's hand. Dad was grinning now and he called through to his wife.

"Joe was making me laugh.. he was telling me about Bob Hills."

Mam came through with some leftovers in a bowl.

"Is that Bob the Tramp?"

"That's him." Dad chuckled before continuing "He was in the Delaval Arms the other night ranting and raving. He reckoned he'd been set upon by ghosts."

Ben's ears pricked.

"Apparently he'd been dossing down in the mausoleum..."

Ben quickly found some string for a lead and went straight to Hylton to tell him the news. The three of them walked to the Avenue Head and watched the horses drinking from the cast iron trough. In time they would laugh about their adventures but not yet. Hylton still shivered at the thought.

"Even Wilson never saw anything as horrible as that werewolf. I haven't been able to sleep. I see that face every night."

As if in mockery, Harvey Hook's voice was ringing out with 'Tell me the Old Old Story'. When Harvey finished his hymn he wandered over to the lads, patted the dog and asked its name.

Ben looked at his friend then put an arm around Hylton's shoulders.

"I think we'll call him Wizard."

And they both cuddled the dog.

Tom Humphrey Seaton Sluice

TO BE CONTINUED...

Drugs?

They say there's a major drug problem in Blyth. Maybe there is, but where?

I live in Blyth, so do my friends, and we have seen nothing of this problem.

Yet it is tarnishing the image of the town.

People like to generalise and blow things out of proportion.

They think drugs affect all areas of the community but it's not true.

I have never seen any needles in the High Street, or smoked out joints in the market square.

Where are the shady dealers with their inside pockets full of illicit substances?

I've never been offered anything.. ever.

The main drugs in the town are cigarettes and alcohol; they always have been.

Outsiders say we are the 'Drug Capital of Northumberland' but since Blyth has the largest population in the county it is not surprising that there are more users here. That still doesn't make it a hotbed for addicts.

No one can deny there have been some tragic local deaths from drug 'cocktails' but Blyth is not a Manchester or a Bradford, and it never will be, I'm pleased to say.

John Diston

Sixth Form, Blyth Ridley High School

> Jonathon Edwards, international triple jumper, held a Fit for Life session with pupils of Blyth Wensleydale Middle School. [*May 1993*]

Jobs?

Unemployment is not pleasant. Many of my friends are without work but they don't choose to be. Blyth and the surrounding area has a strong pull - we like it here for all its faults. Most of the young people I know, have left the town at some time or other, perhaps going south to work in bars or pizza houses. But they are not content and low-paid work, away from home, barely allows them to exist. They give it a try but many come home to their family and friends, hoping to find something locally.

There are some very talented and well-qualified people on the dole and it is not their fault that their skills are not wanted. We are told it is the 'economic climate'. It took me a few years to realise this and to recognise that the problem was not with my attitude, but in circumstances beyond my control. I am still out of work but I no longer feel guilty when I receive my giro. I am comfortable with myself and I feel I have self-worth. I am optimistic about the future, whatever it holds, and maybe the town will once more generate the need for a hard-working and conscientious work force. When it does, the grandsons and granddaughters of all those shipyard workers, miners and railwaymen will be ready and willing to bring renewed prosperity to Blyth Valley.

Andy Treadwell BRIC, Blyth

CHANGING TOWN

Returning to Blyth
Three years away
In the Bus Station
Back home to stay?

Surprising new building
What's this, The Keel Row?
Shops under shelter
From rain, sleet or snow?

But that is the site
Where the church used to be
A new kind of service
With burgers and tea?

In many more shops
The items are cheap
So unemployed pockets
Don't dig quite so deep?

Yet people don't alter
I'm happy to say
They'll stop for a word
Any time of the day.

In the City of London
Where jobs aren't so rare
There's rushing and bustling
With no time to spare.

There's no human contact
They don't meet your eye
In the tube, on the street
They hurry on by.

They seem discontent
They're not satisfied
I notice the difference
In my South-North bus ride.

I'm glad to be back
And one thing I know
I can look up my friends
Of three years ago.

There's a spirit in Blyth
That London finds strange.
It's a pride in belonging
That no-one can change.

Paul Whitfield BRIC, Blyth

A recent OFSTED school inspection reported that an unprecedented 99% of parents at Eastlea First School in Cramlington were more than happy with the quality of education that their children were receiving. [*October 1996*]

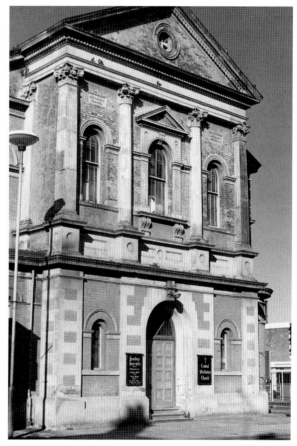

Central Methodist Church, demolished 1990

The Northumbrian Tourist Board announced at their AGM that the region (including Blyth Valley) had achieved a staggering increase of 23% in visitors over the previous year. The Chairman maintained: "The greatest assets of this area are not its hills and history, but its people, their pride and their capacity to work together... it is now up to all of us to convey that special pride of Northumbria as a contemporary region full of diversity and excellence – but proud of its roots".
[*October 1996*]

'The best local authority environmental initiative in the country'. This was how the work of CONE was described at a ceremony in London's Cafe Royal when the Cramlington group received the prestigious Green Initiative award for 1993/94.
[*December 1994*]

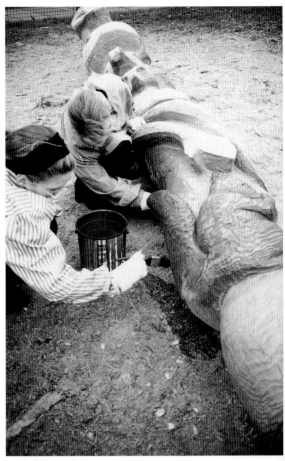

CONE Totem Pole 1996

Wasteland

When I was ten I used to go with my dad and brother to an overgrown wasteland which was situated about a mile down the road between Spar and Westward Grange. Sometimes we stayed for four hours. If it was sunny we would take a packed-lunch and stay even longer. We would all be really tired when we got home because it was such a long way to walk.

We went to look for rabbits and to soak up the environment and get to know about nature. Luckily we are still able to do this as the land has been preserved by a nature group called CONE (Cramlington Organisation for Nature and the Environment). CONE was launched in October 1991 by Blyth Valley Borough Council and has already won several awards for its environmental work. I hope they continue preserving areas such as the wasteland, that hold so many childhood memories for me.

Louise Baird Age 12

Brockwell Middle School, Cramlington

Blyth Windmills

On the 22nd of December I went inside a wind turbine at Blyth Harbour. There are three control positions. Position one is switched off. Position two means the box on top of the windmill will turn around and position three is a manual operation.

Simon the engineer said to me 'Do you want to climb up the windmill?'

I said 'Great!'

It took us twenty minutes to climb up to the top. I felt funny and nervous. Once on top you can control the whole thing.

To make power there are nine wind turbines and they are built on the 100-year-old East Pier. You are not allowed to go onto the pier because of its age. Only the windmill engineers and the Harbour Master can walk along it. In four weeks the windmills can generate enough electricity for 6,000 houses. Each wind turbine has 11,000 volts. Every month the engineer has to check each windmill and tighten the bolts. One more thing, NEVER OPEN the bottom DOOR on the windmill. They are the most dangerous things on the pier.

I have been in the pilot boat twice and I went out to look at the lighthouse. It was rusty on one side but the rest of it was white. I saw workmen putting scaffolding around the lighthouse when it was being painted. At night the lighthouse flashes four times then stops for four seconds.

Behind Cambois Pier there is a wrecked ship. It has been there for 40 or 60 years. The cabin and the anchor have gone but the rest of the boat is still there. If you want to see the boat, go to the Harbour Master's office and get some tide tables. They cost 40p for a year. It is best to go when there is an off-shore wind or a light south but keep a very good eye on the tide. It may trap you. If you do get trapped, always walk along the bottom of the pier.

Daniel Swaddle age 8

Blyth Kingsway First School

Blyth's Euro-Seas centre is at the forefront of world subsea technology. Developments at the old shipyard site will ensure that Blyth's facilities and expertise will attract much of the estimated £4 billion market that will become available in the UK over the next four years. [*July 1996*]

Seaton Delaval Hall

Best Kept Secret

I was just thinking the other day that if you were to stand in the middle of Seaton Delaval roundabout, you would be within reach of some of the best places in the North of England.

I don't know a better fish and chippy and the health food shop is regularly featured on television. Next to our beautiful flower shop, the Crescent Cafe sells the region's best ice-cream; and that's official, they've got a cup!

Down the Avenue is John Vanbrugh's Delaval Hall which is one of the finest houses of its kind in England.. let alone the North East. Next to it is the lovely old Norman church which is the oldest building in the Borough.

Holywell is one of the prettiest villages; it was runner up for a 'Europe in Bloom' competition a few years back and their nature reserve is a really restful spot. The dene and our enviable coastline is on the doorstep and you can be walking on the Cheviot Hills in less than an hour by car.

Where we live is one of the best kept secrets but sometimes I don't think we appreciate what we have got. When our southern relations come here I like showing off where we live. They are amazed and wonder why we don't sell ourselves better. I tell them to keep quiet because we don't want to be overrun. I like it as it is.

Margaret Williamson Seaton Delaval

Jean Bell of the Keel Row Shopping Centre is the first Chair of a new organisation, Blyth Pride. Blyth Pride aims to form a partnership between local businesses, churches, community groups, Northumbria Police and Blyth Valley Borough Council to help make 'a better, friendlier and more prosperous town for everyone to shop and live in'. [*August 1995*]

Golden Windows

When I read contemptuous words about Blyth and the life here I think of 'The House with the Golden Windows'. This is a story I was told as a child at Sunday School:

Once upon a time there was a man who lived in a comfortable house on a hill near a river valley. Most mornings when he got up he saw across the valley a house like his own, but it had golden windows and he longed to live there, despising his own ordinary house. He decided to go and see if the house was for sale.

One morning, as the sun rose behind his house, he set out on his horse to ride around the head of the valley to see the house he admired so much, because he knew he could do the journey in a few hours.

He arrived at the house in mid-afternoon, but there were no golden windows - in fact the net curtains were not as crisp as those at his own house and the windows were not so clean!

Then he turned back to look across the valley at his own home, and as the sun was moving towards its setting in the west, the windows of our hero's house were glistening golden.

I was born in Blyth in 1915 and apart from four years (1933–37) I have lived and worked here all my life. I've always found plenty of 'golden windows' in Blyth – more than broken and dirty ones.

Jean Reid Blyth

From Blyth to Seaton Sluice and back. Ferguson's Sands Race enters its 37th year

ACKNOWLEDGEMENTS

I would like to thank:

Joan Armstrong, Eileen Parker, Mark Annis, Sally Bird and the staff at Cramlington, Blyth and Bedlington Station Libraries.

Northumberland County Council Education Department and in particular Bill Maxwell at Brockwell Middle School, Vic Swift and Matthew Plenty at Eastlea First School, Liz Donaldson at Cambois First School, John Reeves at Ridley High School, Doreen Burnett at St Peter's Middle School, Liz Bangs at Blyth Kingsway First and Joan Scott of East Hartford School.

The history society at Blyth and Cramlington's 'Yesterdays' group.

Blyth's excellent historian, Bob Balmer.

Thanks also Janice Irving at BRIC, Kerrey Ward and the Blyth Harbour Commission, Open Door, Cramlington's 'Yesterdays' group, Blyth Valley Disabled Forum, the Northumbria Disabled Writers and the News Post Leader for permission to use extracts from Blyth News.

Special individual thanks to:

Roger McDonald for the fine art work and stimulating conversations.

Blyth's excellent historian, Bob Balmer.

'Tot' Allan, for allowing me access to his his photographic archives.

The late Norman Arthur of East Hartford; my first contact.

Pat Griffin for her patience and tolerance.

Finally to Helen Payne, who, on behalf of Blyth Valley Council, gave invaluable suggestions, encouragement and commitment to bring 'A Slice of Life' to fruition.

Andy Griffin

Bath Terrace, Blyth